Fitting Form to Function

A Primer on the Organization of Academic Institutions

by Rudolph H. Weingartner

AMERICAN COUNCIL ON EDUCATION ★
ORYX PRESS ★
Series on Higher Education
1996

The rare Arabian Oryx is believed to have inspired the myth of the unicorn. This desert antelope became virtually extinct in the early 1960s. At that time several groups of international conservationists arranged to have 9 animals sent to the Phoenix Zoo to be the nucleus of a captive breeding herd. Today the Oryx population is nearly 1000, and over 500 have been returned to the Middle East.

© 1996 by American Council on Education and The Oryx Press
Published by The Oryx Press
4041 North Central at Indian School Road
Phoenix, Arizona 85012-3397

Published simultaneously in Canada
Printed and Bound in the United States of America

∞ The paper used in this publication meets the minimum requirements of American National Standard for Information Science—Permanence of Paper for Printed Library Materials, ANSI Z39.48, 1984.

Library of Congress Cataloging-in-Publication Data
Weingartner, Rudolph H. (Rudolph Herbert)
    Fitting form to function : a primer on the organization of academic institutions / Rudolph H. Weingartner.
        p. cm. — (American Council on Education/Oryx Press series on higher education)
    Includes bibliographical references and index.
    ISBN 1-57356-022-7
    1. Universities and colleges—United States—Administration.
2. Education, Higher—United States—Decision making. I. Title
II. Series.
LB2341.W426   1996   95-49762
378.1'00973—dc20   CIP

In memory of
Fannia Weingartner
1929–1994
my wife and best friend
for nearly forty-two years

CONTENTS

PREFACE

This book is concerned with the organization of colleges and universities. It was written in the conviction that a thoughtful consideration of this topic can make for more effective institutions. Higher education faces huge problems—inadequate funding, political intrusions, confusion about goals, less than ideal personnel. Whatever insight might be found in these chapters will in no direct way solve any of these problems. Nevertheless, whenever an institution functions more effectively, its ability to accomplish its mission and tackle obstacles increases. Accordingly, I hope this book will be of use not only to administrators of institutions of higher education and to members of their boards of trustees, but also to faculty members and members of the lay public who care about the working of these vital institutions.

My concern is with *organization*, how administrators in the academy should be related to each other and how faculty members might be organized to participate fruitfully in making the institution's decisions. I do not take up this topic by surveying the practices of numerous institutions and reporting which of them have or have not worked. Instead, I consider the *functions* that different decision makers are meant to perform and look at some of the *processes* that are suited to carrying out these functions—themes that serve as the context for my discussion of organizational issues.

Instead of citing empirical research as the basis of what I have to say, I try to justify my suggestions by means of various types of generalizations. While these underpinnings are of course rooted in practice—my own and that of others—the generalizations take the form of observations about the ways of the academy and the world, or of behavioral rules of thumb. I found it worthwhile to elevate some of these principles to the level of Maxim, especially (but not only) when a precept has application in more than one context.

This manner of proceeding has an important advantage for me. The reasons I give for doing something one way rather than another might persuade a reader and, if we're both right, lead him or her to make some improvement. But readers who are not convinced by my words—and this is what I want to focus on—are apt to pit *their* reasons against mine, thus generating the beginnings of a debate. I want, above all, to help members of the academy become more self-conscious about the issues raised in this book and to think harder about them than most of us do most of the time.

I make no attempt to produce a *Compleat Prymer* that covers all aspects of all types of academic institutions. While I try to be relevant both to small colleges and large universities, I do not talk about everything that is to be found in any of them. More specifically, I do not deal with the organization of boards of trustees or regents, nor with the relationship of a campus to the central headquarters of a system of which it might be a part. For a number of reasons, including the considerable literature on boards of trustees, I go only as far "up" as the president, the subject of Chapter 1.

Moreover, I make no attempt to deal with every aspect of the positions and topics that I take up. Instead, I try to give special attention to issues I think to be of particular significance. Thus, in Chapter 1 on the president, I worry about the doability of that job; in the discussion of a faculty senate, I particularly attend to the problem of faculty participation in decision making; when writing about the role of the provost, I try to achieve some clarity about the difference in academic administration between the level of dean and academic vice president.

The book has no footnotes of any kind, since I was not able to find either surveys or other studies sufficiently relevant to make it worth interrupting the reader's momentum. This doesn't mean that I haven't learned much from others, especially from practitioners in different institutions. Of course, numerous recommendations in this book will originally have come to my attention by way of observation at some particular place. I do not, however, identify such places—even where my memory doesn't fail me—and hope that I will be forgiven for that omission. The cheerful side of the same coin is that I also do not point to the institutions from which I learned what *not* to do in this or that situation, lessons that were at least as valuable as the positive ones.

In any case, I often say what most everybody already knows. I do so not only because I think that those everybodies just happen to be right, but, more importantly, because of my stated mission to increase self-awareness. Simply *having* knowledge does not always lead one to *act* upon that knowledge. Perhaps spelling these ideas out explicitly can contribute to shortening the distance between thought and action.

I want to thank my friend James J. Sheehan, the Dickason Professor of Humanities at Stanford University. He read an almost-final draft of this book and both made a number of helpful suggestions for the amplification of the book's content and identified numerous places where my formulation needed improvement. I tried to do justice to his comments; it's not his fault if I didn't always make it. One of the publisher's anonymous readers also had constructive advice, and the Oryx editor, John Wagner, suggested numerous improvements. I benefitted from both in preparing the final version now before the reader.

I am immensely grateful for the constant and thoughtful support I have had from my son Mark and his friend Shannon and from my daughter Eleanor and her husband Miguel. It was during an extended visit to the latter, in Mexico City, that I was able to get back to work on this book and where, later, many of the final revisions were made.

Finally, I am greatly indebted to the Rockefeller Foundation for granting me a stay at its Bellagio Study and Conference Center. The director at the Villa Serbelloni, Pasquale Pesce, and the assistant director, Gianna Celli—together with the staff and our fellow residents—made that stay a most productive one. But much more important, the people there, the setting, and the Villa's matchless ministrations made my wife's and my stay at the shores of Lake Como a last wonderful memory of a life together, since she died unexpectedly soon after our return to the United States. This book is dedicated to her memory.

PRELIMINARIES

THE SPECIAL NATURE OF ACADEMIC INSTITUTIONS

The function of administration, in the academy as elsewhere, is to make decisions and to ensure that they are carried out in the way intended. Good administering means making good decisions and having them effectively expressed in actions; good decisions conform to institutional goals and are rooted in trustworthy and relevant knowledge. Because good decisions must also embody judgments that cohere as a collectivity because they are in accord with policies that transcend any particular decision, the formation of broader policies is also a part of the administrative enterprise.

"Good people make good decisions" is a powerful truism no institution can afford to ignore, but *how* decisions are made and carried out also has a decisive influence on *what* is done. Further, the processes by which institutions function are in turn grounded in the ways in which decision makers and actors are *organized*, how they are deployed to do their work. The organization of academic institutions is the central topic of this book, which rests on the modernist conviction that form should follow function. Accordingly, our inevitable discussions of purposes and processes are intended, above all, to shed light on organization, on how the people in one office are appropriately related to the people in other offices.

Process and organization are more than means to good decisions. In academic institutions, making decisions in the right way also matters for its own sake. One reason for this concern with the way decisions are made is shared with decision making in most non-academic contexts.

Available information and knowledge seldom point to a single right or best course of action, leaving room for "judgment"—that is, for an element of arbitrariness. Moreover, most situations are sufficiently complex to leave room for disagreement by those who are affected by a given decision. When the *rightness* of a proposed action lacks confidence-inspiring obviousness, conviction and legitimacy must be derived from the appropriateness of the *way* in which the decision was reached. For such epistemological reasons alone, using a suitable decision-making process can become part of what it *means* to make a good decision, with procedure conferring its virtue on the outcome.

Some reasons for the significance of the process and organization of decision making are more specific to colleges and universities. Academic institutions are complex in ways in which even such a huge corporation as General Motors is not. For a business, however enormous, an overarching purpose integrates the particular goals of its units and divisions: the maximizing of profit over time. Like everyone else, corporations operate under numerous constraints—of morality, legality, and safety, to name some obvious categories—and must use judgment to make decisions when indubitable knowledge is unattainable. Nevertheless, the activities of individuals and corporate divisions can at least in principle be measured by the contribution they make to the supervening institutional aim.

The mission of colleges and universities, by contrast, is composed of a multiplicity of goals, few of which—however they may be *related* to others—can simply be regarded as *means to, conditions for,* or *components of,* the others. All academic institutions, not just large universities that Clark Kerr termed multiversities, perform many distinct functions. Teaching, the first function, is not in itself a single type of goal. Deep differences exist between the activities (and their institutionalization) required to impart basic knowledge and to teach highly specialized or advanced knowledge, which differs, in turn, from instruction that prepares students for entrance into such professions as law or medicine. Next, academic institutions engage in research, a term that refers to a large cluster of activities that might also be divided into institutionally distinct types. ("Pure" and "applied" research would be examples, although to be clear about such distinctions would require more of a digression than is here needed or justified.) Creative activities are also of diverse genres. Further, colleges and universities provide facilities and activities for the lives of students outside the classroom, and have certain goals regarding their alumni and the surrounding community, including the entertainment of thousands at athletic contests. These and other activities constitute or generate goals that would coexist uneasily under the best of circumstances. In the academy, the constraints of scarce resources and the clash of competing ideologies make controversy inevitable.

This account of the goals of academic institutions could alone explain why the acceptability of decisions is to a degree dependent on the participation of different constituencies in making them. But another complexity cuts deeper still; it is rooted in the distinctive roles that important members of institutions of higher education play at their institutions. First, and central to the matter of an institution's governance, are the members of the faculty. In their faculties, colleges and universities harbor practitioners of diverse professions, who import into their institutions not only the methods and practices of those different professions, but even their goals.

The objectives of engineers at General Motors are set by General Motors. Their assignment includes, among other aims, a determination of what kind of cars they will work on, what these cars should cost to produce, and when they will be ready for the market. The lawyers, economists, accountants, physicians, and numerous other professionals in GM's employ pursue analogous aims. What they are to accomplish is set by the corporation that pays their salaries. The objectives of the professionals on the payroll of a college or university are different. Professors of history, engineering, physics, law, medicine, geology, or philosophy all pursue research goals generated by themselves, even if they have only attained junior rank. The framework—the standards, aims, and mores of the various professions—and the constraints— funding, facilities, fashion, and politics—emanate, with few exceptions, from worlds *outside* the institution that employs them. Thus, as researchers, faculty members have a high degree of autonomy by virtue of the centrality of their association with a profession.

This same relationship also has significant consequences for the role of faculty members as teachers. Yes, the institution that foots the bill makes assignments, although often leaving room for much flexibility. Yes, corporate activity determines requirements, sequences, and the like. But even in basic courses, faculty members have remarkable freedom to determine what they will teach. Again, the influences that limit autonomy have their source in the profession of the teacher, that is, from outside the walls of any particular establishment.

With their central roles so significantly under their own control, faculty members are notably different from corporate employees. The role of faculty members resembles that of independent contractors, even though faculty members also have important tasks in common. Clearly, this fact must bear on the nature of administration at academic institutions. It is the impetus, moreover, for our first maxim, which will often reappear in this book in different contexts: *Maxim 1. In academic institutions, the forces of nature are centrifugal; organizational art must be used to create propensities toward coherence.*

Students also play a special institutional role; although they mostly purchase their educations, students are not just customers. Even those who pay tuition and fees in full, don't pay all their teaching costs; postsecondary institutions must supplement their tuition income with donations, governmental grants, or endowment income—usually with some of all three. Moreover, education is not an ordinary product taken from the seller and used at the buyer's discretion. It is a process that modifies the purchaser permanently, if not always in the ways intended. Still, students are not like hospital patients nor like clients of beauty parlors who, while transformed by the ministrations of these facilities, remain largely passive while others act to change them. By contrast, students must work in lengthy collaboration with their teachers to acquire an education. These characteristics are alone sufficient to give studenthood a special character. Being a student is, then, not like participating in an event, but resembles a mode of life. Where a degree is pursued, undergraduate or graduate, being a student emphatically *is* a mode of life.

I will make no attempt to draw some precise or perfectly general conclusions from these characterizations of faculty and students, but it might be worth putting forward an analogy by way of temporary summary. If one ignores admittedly important economic relationships, both faculty and students bear some resemblance to citizens of a city or country, but in particular the faculty. The citizenship of faculty members—and to a lesser extent of students—stands in contrast to the status of "mere" employees, which resembles that of "mere" subjects of some prerevolutionary Bourbon Louis. Certain rights and obligations to participate in governing flow from the institutional roles of faculty and students; their status and their need for a suitable work environment make such participation both appropriate and necessary. What in the academy is called collegiality becomes analogous to the relationship citizens bear to each other, if perhaps only in a Greek polis or a New England village of yore.

Faculty and students are not the only denizens of colleges and universities; another often large group on campus tends to be referred to by the capacious term of "staff." The meaning here is something like "assistant," with many in this category indistinguishable from employees of conventional business establishments engaged to perform needed tasks: cooks who prepare meals in dining halls, specialists who maintain gardens and roofs, secretaries who fill in forms and type reports, and many more. Others are themselves members of professions—librarians, electronmicroscopists, study counselors, lawyers, and accountants. But because their role is to "assist" faculty and students—directly or indirectly—to carry out their goals, their standing resembles that of professionals in the employ of General Motors more than it does that of a faculty that sets its own goals.

But this resemblance applies to staff only up to a point. Since in place of the corporation's "bottom line," staff members assist in carrying out a variety of *incommensurable* institutional goals, neither the productivity nor the efficiency of staff operations is easily measured. Furthermore, at least one difference between staff members of an academic institution and the employees of a conventional business establishment is both obvious and telling: rather than inhabit a downtown office building, the staff works on a campus and lives cheek by jowl with students and, more importantly, with faculty. The campus, then, is one country, but contains two classes with different stations in life. The presence of these "citizens" and "subjects" is clearly a potential source of tension. If, this side of utopia, the elimination of this disparity seems impossible, prudence alone suggests that some of the rights of citizens simply be accorded to subjects. Because an ethos that fosters the work of faculty and students must characterize an institution in its entirety, it is appropriate for the status of its staff to be somewhat different from the status of employees in most corporations. The staff members of an institution of higher education should, for example, be consulted about their individual assignments and about the practices and plans of the units in which they function.

THE ADMINISTRATION AND DECISION MAKING

Administrators are yet another species of campus dweller. The members of this group do not accomplish any of the missions of their institution;

they do no teach, engage in research, advise farmers how to develop better crops, or guide football teams to victory. Nor do they "assist" in these enterprises in the ways a librarian orders books for students to read or a cook prepares meals for students to eat. The administrator thus cannot simply be regarded as a special category of either the "citizens" (faculty/students) or the "subjects" (staff). We must understand their role, since in the background of all of our discussions lurks a maxim that serves as a kind of institutional Occam's razor: *Maxim 2. Some means cannot be justified by any end; nevertheless, the only way in which a means can be justified at all is by showing that it contributes to bringing about a desired end.*

Administrators manage, an activity that is no more mysterious in the academy than it is in the larger world of business. Whenever the achievement of some goal requires the activities of several or many persons, managers are needed to sequence and coordinate their operations, to ensure that required work is done properly, to correct errors, and to cope with unforeseen incursions. Some people who are called *managers* in the secular world are called *administrators* on a campus. Thus, while staff members do what it takes to register students and maintain a record of their grades, the registrar—the person who manages the department engaged in these operations—is numbered among campus administrators. Similarly, a bursar is not unlike the manager of a department of accounts receivable in the world of business. Indeed, some administrators of this stamp have both titles and functions that are to be found outside the academy, and their incumbents might well have begun their careers in that larger world. To the degree, then, that managing is needed—a matter that can only be decided from case to case—the administrators that do it are a part of the multipartite enterprise that assists faculty and students in carrying out the institution's primary missions.

At the center of this managerial activity is decision making, determining what to do and when and how, together with ensuring that these determinations are carried out. That is how we characterized administering at the outset and, since we are concerned with good and effective decision making, we shall need to consider the proper place of at least some administrators in an institution's organization. Yet, what has so far been said about administrators does not capture the activities of a considerable set of important people: president, vice presidents, deans, and heads and directors. All these officials perform managerial functions, but, as our next maxim illustrates, this fact does not adequately account for the roles they play: *Maxim 3. Academic administrators do not manage units composed of faculty or students, however much they may at times dream of doing so.*

Decision making is still at the heart of the matter of administration, but we must now attend to the special status of faculty members (and, to a lesser degree, of students) and to the enterprise in which they are engaged. Administrators are not merely called upon to *decide*, but to *elicit* decisions from others and to *collaborate* with others in various ways in decision making, with the dual goal of making *good* decisions and doing so in an *appropriate way*. Some types of decisions determine what must be done to carry out effectively the many activities ongoing on a campus; tougher types concern how some of these activities should be changed or eliminated or how new ones should be added; there is also a need to determine what strategies should be used to achieve such goals. A large range of decisions do not simply pertain to one campus operation, but to many or all of them. The move in decision making is from great specificity to a high level of generality, from the narrowly focused to a broader scene, from the consideration of discrete events to the formulation of policy about many; from a concern with the means that bring about the institution's goals to a scrutiny and modification of some of the goals themselves. At some point in this range of decision making it becomes appropriate to speak of leadership, although we will delay a discussion of this topic to the substantive chapters to come.

For the majority of narrowly managerial decisions and even for many of these broader determinations, the appropriate decision-making process involves only members of the administration, although, as we will see, it often matters in what relationship they stand to each other. Even if one were to think away the enormous financial, political, and legal obstacles to a resuscitation of the ancient model that has the faculty of an institution simply administer itself, the thought of it in today's world seems as quaint as driving down a Los Angeles freeway in a horse and buggy—and almost as dangerous. Aside from matters of interest, temperament, and the need to acquire all kinds of knowledge and skills, faculty members would have no time to spare for the activities for which an academic institution exists in the first place. Accordingly, even in the academy with its peculiar characteristics, there are large areas where it is appropriate for decision making to be purely administrative.

But, as one comes closer to the conduct of the academic enterprise itself and to the conditions under which faculty and students go about their business, the need for collaborative decision making arises. Shared *governance* is not, however, a set of prescriptions that formulate just how all academic institutions ought to conduct their ·affairs. It is made up, instead, of a repertory of practices that can vary considerably from institution to institution and during different periods in the history of any one institution. Some of these collaborative practices are indeed formulated in governance documents and bylaws, especially those pertaining to personnel decisions; others remain more fluid. But whether codified or not, these practices are not just ways in which this or that particular college or university happens to do things. Rather, they constitute the manner in which institutions have accommodated, more or less successfully, to their special nature as *academic* institutions, so that, for any given one, the collaborative practices in use are the *appropriate* ones.

While administrators and faculty members can work together in a great many different ways, we distinguish below three broad categories of collaborative decision making. Singling them out will enable us, in the course of this book, to focus on a number of examples, and explore characteristics that enable them to work effectively. The instances singled out in the little typology to follow is of administration collaborating specifically with faculty, rather than with students or staff. Although this combination is of primary concern in this book as the most frequent and fundamental form of joint decision making, there are appropriate occasions for an administration to collaborate with students and staff in analogous ways.

1. *Consultative Decision:* Administrative decisions are appropriately made when the faculty has been *consulted*. The faculty has the least determinative role in this mode of collaboration. This is no doubt the most frequently used, as well as most problematic category. The setting of an institution's budget is a typical example.
2. *Co-determinative Decision:* Administrative decisions are made appropriately when the faculty has given its *advice and consent*. The faculty has a considerably stronger role in this mode of collaborating. In the academy, the most frequent use of this category is in the appointment of administrators.
3. *All-but Determinative Decision:* A decision is appropriately made by (appropriately selected) *faculty members,* subject to *administrative overruling only for strong reasons explicitly stated.* In this mode of collaboration, the faculty has, in principle, the most decisive role, although a number of conditions must be satisfied, if that is also to

be true in practice. A typical example is the process that leads to the promotion of a faculty member.

For the sake of symmetry—and because it is both important and true—one should round out this scheme by noting that just as many decisions are made solely by administrators acting on their own, faculty members—individually and in various groupings—make many decisions without administrative involvement. Indeed, it is possible to gauge the health of an institution by looking at these spheres of relative autonomy. If they are large, with administrators and faculty members making many decisions by themselves *and* (a most important "and"!) complaints about the actions of one party by the other are few, the institution's policies and ethos are likely to be effective and serve as the framework of everyone's decisions.

In the chapters that follow, we will look at a variety of organizational issues in colleges and universities. We will explore the organization of a number of important offices and consider how they are appropriately related to each other, as well as the organization of collaborative decision-making processes. The aim, throughout, is to point to ways in which organizations can contribute both to the quality and the appropriateness of decision making, as this pertains to the particular nature of academic institutions. We begin our examination of these issues with the office of the president.

CHAPTER 1

The President the President's Office

THE FUNCTIONS OF A PRESIDENT

W hen Louis XIV declared that *l'état c'est moi*, he may have had a point, since it is plausible to identify a state with power, something he had in abundance. Yet only confusion and self-deception spring from analogous claims by university presidents, even though such claims are seldom formulated that bluntly. To declare that "I am the college" would imply the falsehood that "I can cause students to learn and knowledge to be created." But *Maxim 2*—which calls for the justification of all means—applies even to chief executive officers. Before we can profitably turn to organizational matters, we must look at what a president does and how a president contributes to bringing about the goals of the institution.

[2] Some means cannot be justified by any end; nevertheless, the only way in which a means can be justified at all is by showing that it contributes to bringing about a desired end.

Providing leadership for an entire institution is the most distinctive presidential function. Only the president is in a position to provide such leadership. Nevertheless, leadership in only one presidential function; there is no such thing as leadership that is divorced from engagement in various institutional processes. Thus the president has wide managerial responsibilities; only the president is so placed as to be able to engage in certain significant external relations; and the chief executive officer of an academic institution—as contrasted with that of a corporation—has pastoral duties to perform vis-à-vis his or her own flock. Such a list of roles assigned to the head of a college or university is alone sufficient support for the frequently made claim that the presidential job is no longer doable. The problem of doability and putative organizational contributions to its solution, in the form of various modes of delegation, are therefore important themes of this chapter.

Brief characterizations of each set of these different presidential assignments only sharpen the question. The performance of presidential *pastoral duties* includes a variety of presidential encounters, formal and informal, with faculty, students, and staff. These encounters acquaint the community with the personality of the person who leads it, with his or her views and style, and especially with his or her beliefs as to what is valuable and worthwhile in the life of the institution. If performed well, these pastoral functions contribute both to the coherence of the institution and to the credibility of its head, providing an opportunity for that person to express concern and even affection for the members of the institution.

If leading the entire institution is the most distinctive function of the president, success in pastoral roles is a vital if not indispensable condition for the exercise of effective leadership. Napoleon's victories on the battlefield, after all, cannot simply be attributed to his tactical and strategic genius, but to the fact that his soldiers loved him and were prepared to follow him even into hell. Translated into the language of chores, an effective pastoral role calls on the president to give formal and informal talks, to hold receptions and to show up at those given by other campus agencies, and to preside over and participate in ceremonies, picnics, dinner parties, and other informal interactions that provide opportunities for the president to speak and *listen* to various campus groups.

External relations refers to the ways in which the president must represent the institution in various off-campus arenas. Many of those external agencies would simply not pay heed to a lesser light. The board of trustees (always) and a system headquarters (sometimes) are external only because in this book we have somewhat arbitrarily drawn the boundary around the institution in a way that leaves them outside it. These supervisory bodies are the sources of numerous mandatory interactions; but there are many others that are not really discretionary. Raising funds for the institution is a principal goal that involves the president with the alumni and with other categories of donors and potential donors. Whether leading a private or public institution, a president must attend to relations with government, a beast with many heads, each one speaking for some branch or level. Further, every institution is placed within a community; a president must interact with its leaders. Finally, no president escapes truck with the media and, through them, with the public at large.

That a president has managerial obligations is best illustrated by the attempt to distinguish between leadership and management. Herewith a summary formulation: to lead is, above all, to set and articulate goals for an institution, while management consists of tending to the manifold and complex processes that bring about institutional goals. But if leadership is not to be confused with prophesy in the manner of the Old Testament, it must also include *moving* the institution towards the *achievement* of those objectives. But it is hard to see how this effort might be accomplished without involvement in those institutional processes. A president is thus confronted by managerial responsibilities, if only because this distinction between leading and managing is nowhere near as sharp as such a simple verbal formulation might make it appear.

Signal examples of managerial activities, conducted at different institutional levels or with greater or lesser specificity, include the selection and supervision of personnel, the formulation of procedures whereby the various subdivisions of an institution go about their business, and the allocation of resources to various sectors. Two formulations can be given to the wobbly leadership-management distinction, the first philosophical and abstract and the second practical and down to earth. Ends, to take the theoretical perspective first, are seldom wholly separate and separable from the means that bring them about. The ladder that can be kicked away once it has led the climber to the roof is not a typical example of the way means work. More usually, means are *contained* in the end, in *how* an end is brought about; the processes that led to its achievement are to a degree contained in the end because they remain among its characteristics. (An appointed Jones, for example, is not the same as an elected Jones. Same person, a different institutional role by virtue of the different means by which the office was attained.) More generally still, we must avoid regarding means and ends as entities of distinctly different kinds, since few ends, if any, are "final." Instead, means and ends are everywhere linked as complex, intertwining chains, with the end of one process becoming one of the means in another.

The practical view is expressed in a common saying: "The devil is in the details." The *devil* lurks there because components have the capacity to vitiate the whole that contains them. When things come out the way we want them to, we are likely to pay little attention to all the elements that led there. But since we become sharply aware of details when things go wrong (for want of a nail a kingdom was lost!), we must recognize the significance of all of the processes for the achievement of institutional goals. Again, the *way* a goal is brought about modifies the goal itself.

These broad considerations show that even when we acknowledge that the central role of a president is to provide leadership to the institution over which he or she presides, the demands of management cannot be avoided and thus add to the presidential burden. While acknowledging the naivete of associating management with means and leadership with ends, we will see below that it becomes all the more important to be able to discern differences of degree between them in a continuum. Managing is found at one end, where the job is that of selecting and manipulating means, within a framework of goals that are taken as given. Leadership activities are those that are concerned with goals themselves. Toward that end of the continuum, the concern is with the determining, rethinking, or reshaping of the frameworks of objectives themselves. In an alternative formulation, managing pertains to the more specific and narrowly focused, while leadership is concerned with the broader picture. However regarded, presidential managing is unavoidable.

The president has much to do, rendering plausible the claim that the job is undoable. But two caveats at the outset. First, what a college or university president's job is like is a function of the way the academic world works at the end of the twentieth century and how the larger world impinges on the academy. Insight into the relationship between the organization of academic institutions and the effectiveness of the presidential office might at best help to ameliorate the plight of the president, with only Don Quixote left to think that such illumination could alter the fundamental situation that causes it.

Second, to claim that the president's job is undoable does not mean that no one does it, but "merely" that at best it can be done *well* only by means of rare and probably self-sacrificial and super-human efforts. The concern with doability, then, raises the issue of the evaluation of presidential performances, requiring that I make explicit a bias that underlies many of the judgments in this book. Assuming the president does such basic things as maintain financial solvency, and that the peculiar histories of institutions generate different needs at different times, I believe presidential performance should be measured by the success with which a president pursues the primary goals of a college or university, supporting and improving those activities that make an academic institution distinctively academic. More weight is thus here given to successes and failures at the goal end of the continuum, to the achievements of leadership over those of management.

THE NATURE OF SUPERVISION AND THE PROBLEM OF AN EXECUTIVE VICE PRESIDENT

I maintain that how an entire academic institution is organized bears on the doability of the president's job. How the president's own office is organized and to whom and how the chief executive officer delegates responsibility has primary relevance. Among conventional institutional devices for lessening the burdens of the president is the appointment of an executive vice president to whom the heads of most of the institution's units report, including the chief academic officer. Since the unrelenting need to placate an ubiquitous devil undermines the ability to lead, the president can concentrate on leadership functions (as well as external and pastoral relations) and essentially turn over the management of the institution to an office created for that purpose.

Perhaps suggested by the model of a corporation, with labor divided between chief executive and chief operating officers, this scheme keeps small the number of people who report directly to the president and pushes that managerial burden onto the shoulders of a specialist installed for the purpose. This strategy rests on the laudable counsel that the highest official of an organization should retain those functions that cannot be delegated, while others take care of those that can be.

Although a plausible solution to a central presidential problem, the creation of an executive vice presidency nevertheless stands a good chance of undermining precisely the goal it seeks to achieve by compromising the centrality of the institution's academic functions. Such an effect would surely be unintended and might remain unnoticed for some time and perhaps always to those inside the institution. This outcome would rest on the interrelated facts that the distinction between leadership and management is blurred, that the end contains the means that brought them about, and that devilish details have consequences for the totality. Turning over mangement and means to an executive vice president might in short, give away more than intended.

A special reason, however, rests on a principle embedded in the following: *Maxim 4. To what position a given officer reports significantly affects the way in which his or her responsibilities are discharged.* First, more or less prestige attaches to different boxes in a table of organization, where higher and lower on the page tends to translate into higher and lower status, as this is perceived both inside an institution and outside it. And since such patterns of boxes can become baroquely complex, the standing (or lack of it) of the official designated by one box rubs off on those who report to him or her, whether as "line" or "staff" officers. Thus, if sometimes the status of the president's secretary is higher than the secretary of a vice president, one can be sure that the prestige of an executive vice president who reports directly to the CEO is greater than that of the chief academic officer who "only" reports to that executive vice president. The mystique of status thus has operational value, even if it is not calculated daily on some big board, where more power—a greater ability to bring about desired goals—is directly related to higher status.

But a second aspect of *Maxim 4* is even more important. Any institutional role embodies a certain bundle of goals, preferences, priorities, and even ways of doing things—all to a degree independent of the person who holds the post. In various ways, this packet impinges, often powerfully, on the persons who report to a given officer and shapes the behavior of these subordinates.

[4] To what position a given officer reports significantly affects the way in which his or her responsibilities are discharged.

Think of the likely difference in the public relations output between that produced by a corporate PR department whose head is supervised by the vice president for manufacturing and one who is overseen by the vice president for marketing. Surely the values and goals of those two different corporate functions would leave their mark on all the advertisements, press releases, and brochures, churned out by departments so differently placed within the corporate structure.

We will meet up again and again with the import of *Maxim 4*, but perhaps nowhere with broader consequences than here. Precisely because an executive vice presidency is created to assume the managerial tasks on the highest institutional level, the executive vice president's main interests become *efficiency and smooth functioning*—no crises, surprises, disturbances or trouble; the managerial *summum bonum* becomes a balanced budget and an absence of strife and negative publicity. This chief operating officer is induced to be fair and even-handed in the treatment of different campus segments and interests, to assume a stance of neutrality aimed at giving equal weight to the voices and needs of all major constituencies. Inevitably, the primacy of the academic enterprise becomes submerged, its activities regarded as one type among others, with the executive vice president unavoidably taking on the role of adjudicator among conflicting claims and insisting on fiscal responsibility above all. To have the chief academic officer report to an executive vice president thus conflicts with the fundamental bias of this book, which insists on the primacy of the academic enterprise.

This strong conclusion drawn from a brief consideration of the *role* of an executive vice president prompts a comment that applies to the rest of this book. The assignment of considerable power to the character of an *office* does not imply that it makes no difference who *holds* the office. An essay such as this operates in the artificial world of *ceteris paribus*, other things being equal, an impossible state in the world in which we live. Office holders are never robots and seldom mere ciphers, so that actual persons and personal relationships affect the ways in which offices are conducted. A particular executive vice president might thus have the disposition to resist the pressure to be even-handed and treat the chief academic officer as first and not merely as one among equals On the other side, even where there is no executive vice president, an actual business vice president might nevertheless exercise the *de facto* power of the higher office, by virtue, say, of a close friendship between vice president and CEO, even though, formally, the chief academic officer reports directly to the president. Personalities and their interrelationships can sometimes sharply modify the expectations built into the organization of offices. However, even in the real world, many things *are* equal, at least in the long run, so that organizational relationships do make a difference.

If there is no executive vice president to whom both the chief academic officer and business-finance officer report, there remain two options. In what might be called a classical ideal, the chief academic officer serves as the chief operating officer of the institution and supervises the officer responsible for budgetary and business affairs, among others. A second organizational alternative may often be more feasible: both the academic head and the business-finance vice president report to the president as organizational equals.

Maxim 4 suggests that having the chief academic officer serve as the institution's chief operating officer will predispose the business establishment to support the academic one. Given the bias of this book, the tail is less likely to wag the dog. This arrangement has the additional advantage of freeing more of the president's time and energy for the external and fund-raising functions no one else can assume. Where such an arrangement works well, the two senior officers will for all practical purposes divide all top executive labors into inside and outside, with the chief academic officer handling the former and the president the latter.

A number of obstacles stand in the way of having this classical design work effectively. On the personal side, clearly a close and easy relationship is imperative between president and chief academic officer, with both "being of one mind" about most things that matter. The absence of such close interactions can lead to many possible calamities that I leave to the reader's imagination or experience to spell out.

More mundanely, in large and complex institutions, where the academic establishment consists of numerous colleges, schools, centers, and facilities, the chief academic officer may simply have too much to do to give adequate supervision to the head of the business-finance operation. The point of having the business vice president report to the academic head could easily be undermined by having the latter pay inadequate attention to the former. Another institutional obstacle to an outside-inside split of top executive functions is directly rooted in conditions that are widespread during the waning years of our century. Balancing the operating budget, managing capital expenses, and maximizing the return on the endowment are often such overriding imperatives and so integral a part of the relationship of president to board of trustees that there is no *practical* alternative to having the president directly supervise the budgetary and business processes of the institution.

For various reasons, then, an institution might reject the orthodox relationship between chief executive and chief operating officer, requiring the president to add the vice president for business affairs to the officers that report to the top office. Indeed, so as to maximize presidential authority, Maxim 4 might well sway a CEO to expand the list of officers he or she supervises. But another principle closely related to the doability of the presidential (or any other) job pushes in the opposite direction: Maxim 5. *Supervising is work, calling for the dedication of time, energy, and know-how.*

[4] *To what position a given officer reports significantly affects the way in which his or her responsibilities are discharged.*

Those thin lines that link the boxes of a table of organization inadequately symbolize the relationships that hold among the people who "occupy" them. To exercise the influence implicit in the notion of *supervising* entails the expenditure of time and effort in a considerable range of activities—from the selection of the person supervised, at one end of the range, to his or her periodic evaluation at the other. Effective supervision, moreover, requires a certain grasp of the issues that confront those who are supervised—another demand for work. In academic institutions, the need to do homework to achieve sufficient comprehension of a large range of issues is particularly great. In the corporate world, persons seldom become chief executive officers without considerable prior administrative experience and the benefit of implicit or explicit grooming. Heads of academic institutions often land in their jobs with much less preparation for the broad responsibilities they incur at the top. To repeat, supervising is work.

Supervising can be done with varying degrees of conscientiousness and specificity. Although I will shortly have something to say about excessive superintendence, a high price is paid for ignoring too many supervisory burdens. Where reporting relations are kept merely nominal, there is apparent supervision without actual oversight. Authority is ceded to an unsupervised administrator, while the supervisor nevertheless retains responsibility. To the subordinate, *de facto* autonomy is given, regardless of what the table of organization might convey. During good times and with good people in office, the result might merely be amiable incoherence—a state of affairs that, for better or for worse, more than one academic institution has had to weather. In recent years, such favorable seas have been rare and brief. And when the waters are rough, incoherence becomes self-destructive.

SUPERVISING: SOME EXAMPLES

Director of Athletics

An awareness of *Maxims 4* and *5*—and of the tension between them— must inform the organizational location, vis-a-vis the president, of administrators for whom *some* reason exists for them to report directly to the institution's head. We cannot here discuss the numerous candidates who might advance such a claim, but will take up

[5] Supervising is work, calling for the dedication of time, energy, and know-how.

two of them in a way that is instructive for the consideration of others. Accordingly, we will address first the location (on a table of organization, that is) of an institution's director of athletics and continue with the head of development.

We will here consider three candidates (among potentially others) to serve as supervisor of the director of athletics—president; chief business officer, such as vice president for business and finance; or the officer who oversees student life. From this consideration, we will derive a sense of the way in which *Maxim 4* works in the context of an academic institution. It will not be hard to see that three different organizational schemes are prone to yield different kinds performances of the athletic director's job, regardless of the reasons and events that led up to the scheme adopted. One would add that the way the assignment is carried out will have more to do with the role of the incumbent's supervisor than with the incumbent's own personality, were it not for the fact that the director of athletics is also selected by the supervisor who seeks to engage a person of the kind that is likely to do the job he or she wants done.

[4] To what position a given officer reports significantly affects the way in which his or her responsibilities are discharged.

The dean or vice president for student affairs must provide a satisfactory life for students on campus—a vague phrase that can be left uninterpreted in the present context. Given such responsibilities, this officer will look to the director of athletics as a collaborator, as someone who will help to carry out this mission. Thus the head of student affairs will engage a person who is likely to make athletics contribute to student life; will, in guiding the work of the director of athletics, encourage and support the incumbent to engage in activities aimed at that goal and discourage those that undermine it; and, finally, will base the evaluation and rewarding of that administrator at least in part on the effectiveness of the contribution to the desired goal.

The vice president for business and finance is charged with assuring that campus units function efficiently and that the institution's budget is kept in balance, whatever the job's full description may be. No doubt this vice president will also want student life on campus to be satisfactory (in whatever sense) but no one who reports to this officer can be excused from contributing to the basic aims of the supervisor. Thus, in hiring, guiding, and evaluating a director of athletics, the business and finance values of the "bottom line" will play a central role, and will likely result in a different performance from a director of athletics reporting to a dean of students.

If the director of athletics reported to the president, his or her performance would differ in other ways. Why should the athletic director report to the president, for neither contributions to student life nor to balancing the budget warrant presidential attention? This organizational scheme casts the director of athletics in the role of special assistant to the president-as-minister-for-external-affairs. It is thus no surprise that athletics often reports to the president in cases where the

institution is engaged in Division I competition or where there is strong
alumni or community demand for the visibility of some of its competi-
tive sports. The president looks to the director of athletics for assistance
with external relations, above all by way of the positive achievement of
team records that meet or exceed the expectations of the institution's
constituency, but also by means of the negative one of keeping the
athletic enterprise free of scandal.

The arrangement is reasonable until one considers the effect of
Maxim 5. When the burdens of supervision are put into the equation,
one is likely to be confronted by the following
dilemma. If, on the one hand, the president takes
those supervisory duties seriously and devotes the
requisite time and energy to the varied problems
of athletics, too much of the chief executive officer's time and energy is
drawn away from activities that are considerably more central to the
institution's mission. If, on the other hand, the reporting is nominal,
considerable autonomy is ceded to the director of athletics. Such absence of oversight can have undesirable consequences, quietly corrupting central academic processes or making noisy headlines in the daily
press. There are powerful reasons, therefore, to consider alternative
reporting lines, even where the realities of Division I competition vie for
primacy with the contribution of athletics to a satisfactory student life
on campus.

[5] Supervising is work, calling for the dedication of time, energy, and know-how.

Director of Development

The organizational location of the head of development raises somewhat different issues. (New titles, such as "vice president for institutional advancement" are now replacing "vice president for development"—either because the older term's euphemistic powers are wearing
off or so as to acknowledge that this officer oversees public relations, in
addition to raising money. I will here stick to the old fashioned and
shorter term.) Academic institutions are required to procure funds from
various sources and the president must see that this goal is pursued.
Because the CEO cannot effectively delegate certain tasks to anyone
below the presidential level, the relationship between president and
head of development is a complex one, permitting us to gain additional
insight into the reporting relationship.

The president needs the *assistance* of the head of development in
fund raising activities which often require these two officers to work in

close cooperation in communicating and interacting with donors. Without claiming that a precise meaning can be given to the term, let us refer to this work of the vice president for development as a *staff* function, since it is largely oriented to carrying out the purposes of the *principal*, the institution's president. Important aspects of the development head's job thus require direct supervision by the CEO. A supervisor *assigns duties* to a staff person to help him or her accomplish certain tasks; authority to set goals or formulate policies is essentially retained by the supervisor. If some joint activity should involve collaborative decision making and call for consultation with the faculty, for example, the responsibility to engage in the requisite process lies with the president, as principal, even if it is delegated to the staff person to seek the appropriate counsel. In this capacity as assistant, the head of development must clearly report to the president.

The head of development also manages an enterprise of many activities, carried out, in larger institutions, by squadrons of staff persons who are specialists in different aspects of fund raising and public relations. Moreover, this labor is not accomplished merely for the sake of assisting with the president's work. The development department serves the needs of other campus divisions, in larger and more complex institutions. As the manager, therefore, of an auxiliary unit—to use one of the traditional labels for an institution-wide service organization—the director of development must be given *authority* to hire and fire personnel, and to devise and execute policies. Indeed, if, as department head, it is appropriate for the development officer to consult with faculty groups or with other administrators, it is that person's responsibility to do so. In this managerial role, then, there is no special reason why the chief of development should report directly to the CEO, any more than must the head of the campus's physical plant.

One qualification to this last statement is worth commenting on because it illustrates one of the special characteristics of colleges and universities pointed out in the Preliminaries. If development were an activity of a business corporation, the success of that department could no doubt be measured simply by the amount of money it brought in, minus the cost of raising it. But the absence of a single bottom line in an institution of higher education makes it necessary to ask for just what *purposes* different sums have been raised and what the relationship is between the mix of functions that are served by development and the goals of the institution. This tension between amount of money raised and the purposes for which it is designated makes supervising the chief of the department of development a difficult matter and in itself worthy of the president's attention.

Nevertheless, the two roles just distinguished—as presidential "assistant" and as department head— point to important differences in the ways in which one person might report to another. As assistant in the president's fund-raising activities, serving as *staff* to the head of the institution, the development director is the president's *agent* in selected activities. As the manager of a department, authority and powers as well as duties are *delegated* to the director of development. The director's job is to accomplish certain institutional goals; it is therefore appropriate that this administrator be given the authority to determine the means to be used and even accorded considerable scope in giving specific shape to those broad aims—within the framework of institutional policies explicitly formulated and cognizant of unstated institutional mores and customs. The difference between the two relationships is like that between an investment *advisor* and an investment *manager*. The former makes recommendations and, when they have been adopted by the assets' owner, executes the agreed-upon transactions. The latter actually makes financial decisions in behalf of the owner—within a framework of policies, broadly or narrowly drawn—and carries them out without further approval by the owner.

The distinction between ways of reporting is important in our context— a fact to be elaborated upon shortly—but the case just now under discussion shows that it is subject to gray areas. There surely is much continuity between the helpmate activities of the director of development and those activities performed as unit head, with concomitant ambiguities about the locus of authority of particular actions. But if a significant number of activities of the head of development are not readily classifiable into one of the two types, a specific implication follows immediately: that officer must report directly to the president. Confusion and conflict would be inevitable, if the development vice president were to collaborate closely with the president in important fund-raising activities while as head of the fund raising establishment he or she reported to someone else.

An important general principle can also be derived from this gray area between line and staff activities, a principle that bears directly on the problem of the doability of the president's job. The differences between the two types of reporting relationships have a tendency to be more obvious to the supervised than to the supervisor. Supervision of both kinds is work; Maxim 5 applies to both, even if there are differences in modes of oversight. In accord with Maxim 4, a supervisor, to be effective in influencing those who report to him or her, must be conscientious in the tasks of oversight, whether the person supervised is a staff member or the head of a unit with considerable autonomy.

[5] Supervising is work, calling for the dedication of time, energy, and know-how.

[4] To what position a given officer reports significantly affects the way in which his or her responsibilities are discharged.

It is possible, however, to carry conscientiousness in supervision to a point where oversight ceases and ventriloquism begins. Both the delegation of the authority to bring about certain goals and the assignment of tasks that assist a supervisor imply that another person does the job, presumably someone endowed with the requisite judgment and skills. But while different situations call for different levels of specificity in the formulation of assignments and for different blends of surveillance and independence, supervision can be taken to such an excess that a person engaged to share in work is converted to a mere instrument. If the lack of all supervision is symbolized by the absence of a line connecting two boxes on an organizational chart, micromanagement, to give this excess a name, comes close to eliminating one of the boxes altogether. While the chart suggests that two (or more) persons are doing the institution's work, the reality of micromanagement has reduced that to one person—a person with a tool.

In this way, any organizational contribution to the doability of a president's job is effectively nullified because the formal scheme is not actually implemented. Moreover, an amusing though superfluous couple of pages could be written about the ways in which a micromanaging supervisor might set about evaluating the performance of a micromanaged subordinate. Whose judgment is being scrutinized? Just who is doing a good job if the work is well done and who is to blame if it is not? Is a thoroughgoing micromanager even capable of assessing simple obedience of the subordinate? The seriousness of such undermining of an institutional design merits the formulation of the following maxim: Maxim 6. If the organizational chart is the right one, and micromanagement exists, either the supervisor or the supervised is the wrong person for the slot.

THE NATURE OF SUPERVISION AND THE DOABILITY OF THE PRESIDENT'S JOB

Having sketched out accounts of the use and misuse of two types of reporting relationships, we can apply them more directly to the problem of the doability of the president's job. Even though the distinction between staff relationships and those in which authority is ceded is not at all clean—especially in the absence of such props as the legal and contractual framework that functions in the world of finance—it has a useful place in the academy. Recall our earlier characterization of faculty members, the leading inhabitants of academic institutions, as requiring a special kind of independence if they are to do their job. If they were left solely to their own devices, the risk is chaos; the need for administration has all along been conceded, if only for the sake of institutional coherence and coordination among various faculty groupings.

But there is also the analogy of citizens in a free society, who thrive best in a setting that allows considerable autonomy to individuals. In a similar way, faculty members work most effectively in an environment in which substantial authority is ceded to them by those who govern. Indeed, there is a fatal conflict between a controlling, hierarchical mode of administration and an administered faculty whose role requires considerable scope for action. In some instances, the needed autonomy is simply smothered by the regimenting network of rules and regulations that is the inevitable expression of a supervisory system that fails to transmit authority to lower levels. In other cases, however, such an accumulation of bureaucratic directives does not stifle—simply because the faculty develops practices that circumvent them.

Such avoidance of the effects of regimentation might be regarded as a sign of the health of the academic enterprise, preserving itself, in Darwinian fashion, in spite of a hostile environment. But the price for such survival tends to be high. Some scope for faculty action is preserved in these rare instances by evasive and devious tactics that are wasteful of time and energy and frequently corrupting of faculty-administration relations. Just as all laws are undermined in what one might call an unsuccessfully oppressive society, so the practices that enable academics to play their roles within a stifling bureaucracy is likely to render epiphenomenal many of the institution's regulations—good, bad, and indifferent.

The complement, then, to an open-textured, decentralized organization, at least of the institution's academic enterprise, is a reporting
scheme in which authority is delegated downward from the chief executive officer to chief academic officer and further. The choice of the
persons to whom authority is delegated is thus a paramount managerial
task for a chief executive, equaled only by the allocation of resources to
those on whom that authority is conferred. In contrast with a more
tightly knit hierarchical organization, much less flows upward for substantive approval and ratification by the highest officer. Nevertheless,
vital duties of supervision remain, mostly in conversational form. Supervisor and supervised inform and persuade each other on broad goals and
directions, on a delineation of priorities, and on a sense of the standards
the institution will aim to follow in various of its activities. The outcome
will either be reasonably close to agreement or spell trouble. Inevitably,
these envisaged dialogues must make reference to specific persons,
cases, and events, for our language tends to make vague, if not downright vapid, most abstract discussions of goals, priorities, or standards.
But if authority is to be truly delegated, the crucial role of such specific
instances is to point more effectively to those difficult-to-express ab-
stractions, with the understanding that there is always a plurality of ways
in which a given set of goals might be reached.

Some readers on reading the last few paragraphs, will note that many
state systems or boards of trustees do not permit the kind of decentralization in which "much less flows upward for substantive approval and
ratification." Yet, even in such circumstances, this paradigm is relevant.
In the real world, we must fashion compromises in the face of laws,
regulations, and influential persons beyond the control of a given campus. In that world, good government is served by the awareness of what
reality might be better, for such self-consciousness will help to prevent
giving up more than the circumstances demand.

THE DOABILITY OF THE PRESIDENT'S JOB AND THE USE OF STAFF

If, in a decentralized academic setting, the chief executive tends to be
less involved in day-to-day management, the need for a president to
exercise leadership by influencing the enterprises of the institution in
indirect ways is even greater. But in order to articulate institutional
goals in an ongoing way and to express as well as to contribute to
refashioning an institution's ethos, a CEO must, in an equally ongoing
way, communicate, face-to-face, with numerous individuals and groups

belonging to all campus constituencies—faculty and students, above all. The point of such interactions is not to bypass the existing administrative structure, but to have the president informed, on the one hand, about campus activities and mood, and to provide opportunities, on the other, for him or her to give expression to institutional goals in informal, but specific ways. Even in an army, the commanding general does not communicate with his troops only through his staff; how much more obvious that the head of an academic institution must learn first hand from "constituents" and influence them directly.

The need to administer these interactions is alone a reason to make use of a staff person, either modestly designated "assistant to the president" or, more formidably, "chief of staff," depending on the size and complexity of the institution and of the president's office. More generally, the use of staff can contribute toward making the CEO's job doable without enlarging the institution's bureaucracy by allowing the president to perform managerial tasks through the agency of one or more such assistants. The office of the president—in an extended sense of the term—is thus enlarged, without the addition of further layers of authority.

Supervision in these relationships amounts to the assigning of tasks—varying in magnitude from representing the president at certain meetings to organizing the search for an important administrator. All these are carried out by the staff member, not on his or her own authority, but "in the name of " the principal. The more suitable the persons selected for such close relationships, the less burdensome the overseeing of their work. For good sense, together with the understanding that is fostered by frequent informal interactions, progressively reduces the need to spell out how an assignment is to be accomplished. In such cases, however, we are not speaking of delegating the authority to select means—which brings with it the concomitant power to affect the character of the end—but of the assistant's understanding as to the ways in which the president wants such responsibilities discharged.

Here again, an organizational method of accomplishing needed tasks works only to the extent to which the occupants of those boxes play the roles assigned to them. On the one side, micromanagement comes close to nullifying the labor-saving advantages of a staff appointment. Still, it is the lesser of two distortions, since the only person who directly suffers from it is the person whose burdens were meant to be lightened. But inadequate supervision, or the choice of the wrong person, can give independent authority to a person intended to be staff and thus add a layer to the bureaucracy, whatever the organizational chart might say. A need would be created to appeal from a staff action to the president, rendering decision making more cumbersome, an effect that is all the more unfortunate because the additional layer is unacknowledged or downright surreptitious.

Finally, the concept of "assistant to the president" is fruitfully extended to officials who engage in various more specialized pursuits. The institution's counsel is plausibly thought of as a special assistant to the president, as well as the secretary of the college or university, where institutional size and complexity warrant a distinct office. Where needed, specialists, in community or governmental relations are usefully considered to be such assistants, even though they, like counsels, serve other units on campus besides the president and may, at least in larger institutions, head sizeable offices of their own. In different ways, counsels and officials engaged in community or governmental relations make important specialized contributions to the way different external publics regard their institutions and, less directly, constituencies within the institution.

Since conducting external relations and sustaining an institutional ethos are both significant and difficult presidential responsibilities, direct supervision of such officials increases the likelihood that their work assists rather than hampers the chief executive officer in creating conditions that make leadership possible. Supervision, moreover, should largely be limited to a formulation of the goals to be achieved. Since bringing these goals about calls for technical knowledge and skill, the devil in the details is either successfully tamed by the specialists engaged to do the job or other specialists must be brought in to replace them. Again, the doability of the president's task is furthered, not by micromanagement, but by the sort of supervision that communicates clearly what is to be done and insists that the goals set are accomplished.

One way a president is kept busy is in interaction with the campus faculty as organized for collaborative decision making. In the next chapter, we discuss the senate and some of its committees, paying particular attention to two related issues crucial to the effectiveness of such collaboration: the problem of faculty participation in governance activities and the difficulties that beset the consulting process.

CHAPTER 2

Collaboration and Consultation: The Central Administration and the Faculty

THE NEED FOR A SENATE

W e've just finished treating the college or university president as if that officer were the top administrator of a corporation. But we know from our introductory discussion of the special character of academic institutions that not all decisions are made solely by the CEO or other authorized administrators, and that the president speaks on some issues only after interacting with other campus constituencies, especially the faculty. Much collaboration between administration and faculty or students takes place in specialized settings, with different administrative officers working together with groups of faculty or students to jointly accomplish specific tasks. In Chapters 6 and 7, we will look in some detail at the organization of collaborative decision making of the third category (see "Preliminaries"), in which the role of the faculty is all but determinative. In this chapter, we discuss collaborative decision making at the all-campus level and put into focus, as the counterpart to the president, a campus-wide organization such as a senate.

Neither the usefulness of nor the need for such an organization may be obvious, and its workability may be problematical, especially in the light of the following maxim: *Maxim 7. Specificity in the formulation of a task fosters the effectiveness of collaboration in carrying it out.* For if this maxim is true, why not parcel out particular issues to committees that are formed for the purpose of dealing with them—groups that will then collaborate with appropriate administrators and get on with their tasks together? Such advice is indeed sensible; but even where it is followed, the need for that global body does not go way. Some issues clearly affect everyone, such as the way in which funds are allocated or what is planned for the institution's future. The effects of other issues are less clear, although even those pertaining *primarily* to some subgroup on campus also impinge on the rest of the community. Because a price tag, obvious or hidden, attaches to virtually all decisions, we can express the next maxim as follows: *Maxim 8. Few significant campus decisions are without budgetary implications.* What is spent for your cause cannot be spent for mine. But even ignoring the ubiquity of economics, the effect of apparently circumscribed decisions on the institution as a whole is equally pervasive. Decisions about parking or admissions policies, about intercollegiate athletics or about requiring a foreign language have ramifications beyond the people immediately concerned. This is true, if only because decisions characterize the institution of which everyone is a member.

Your business may not be my business, but what each of us does modifies *our* college or university. However, this reality does not prevent each province from *aiming* to pursue its interests as it alone sees fit, which recalls *Maxim 1.* Whatever coherence-mak-

[1] *In academic institutions, the forces of nature are centrifugal; organizational art must be used to create propensities toward coherence.*

ing artifices presidents and other administrators can muster must be complemented by an organization that speaks for the campus as a whole.

In times of crisis, having an organization such as a senate becomes a necessity. Especially at such moments, administrators acting on their own are inadequate as spokespersons for the policies and interests of the institution. The participation of a senate can help shape positions that pertain to the entire institution and confer upon them a legitimacy that is relevant both to the members of the institution and to the world outside it.

Whether in peaceful times or turbulent, the agency that speaks for the whole institution may be a senate, faculty council, assembly, or the faculty meeting in its entirety. Which of these and under what circumstances will be considered below; until then, the term "senate" will stand for any one of them. Before describing specific assemblies, we must discuss what it takes for any version of an all-campus organization to do its job.

CONDITIONS FOR A SENATE'S EFFECTIVE FUNCTIONING

To concede the need for a senate does not overcome the widespread doubt that such a body can function well. The symptoms of governance malaise are all too familiar. The number of faculty members who take part in senate and committee deliberations is usually small relative to the number eligible to do so. Moreover, the same faces appear and reappear among the participants, with few being the campus's most successful scholars and teachers. The faculty comes to regard governance activities as the province of mere politicians, who speak for themselves only and are therefore unable to overcome centrifugal forces. At the same time, cynicism becomes the symptom among administrators. They go through the motions of collaborative decision making because bylaws or good politics require it, but they have no respect for these processes and pay as little heed to them as is compatible with a sullen peace.

Inadequate participation is a central problem here, and, like voter apathy in civil society, this condition is not easily alleviated. Given what draws people into academic careers in the first place, it is not surprising that many faculty members prefer spending their time in studies and laboratories, rather than in conference rooms of committees. The belief that faculty members have better things to do than go to meetings is then reinforced by the disproportion between time and effort there expended and the results accomplished. Improvement can be achieved by resolutely attending to the following maxim: *Maxim 9. The number and quality of persons who participate in governance activities are directly related to how effectively they influence conditions that matter to them.*

Such effectiveness is dependent on two conditions. First, it matters what the group does: what topics it deals with, how important they are, what the quality is both of its deliberations and of the conclusions it reaches. Second, it matters what happens to those conclusions: to what avail does the group work, what comes to pass in the real world as a consequence of its efforts? Before examining how organizational considerations bear on the internal aspects of the effectiveness of committee work, we will first take up the relationship between governance activities and the actual life of the institution.

This topic takes us to the heart of administration/faculty collaboration in decision making. The second and third modes of collaboration (see "Preliminaries")—the co-determinative and the all-but determinative—provide some assurance of external effectiveness. Where both administration and faculty group must agree on the action to be taken, such as in the selection of an administrator, faculty collaborators can expect to have their work impinge on the course of events at their institution. The scheme that calls for the acceptance of what a faculty has resolved—except where an administration is prepared to provide a strong reason to the contrary—is adopted on the assumption that such a veto will be infrequent. While neither of these modes of joint decision making is immune to an institutional breakdown that would render the collaborative activity ineffectual, they both have features that make collaboration likely to work.

The same cannot be said about the most prevalent mode of collaboration, that in which an administration first *consults* the faculty before making a decision. The frequency with which consultation malfunctions is probably the single largest cause of governance malaise. The topics taken up by a senate or committee may have been just the ones everyone thought to be important; the deliberations may have been thorough and well conducted; and the recommendations arrived at may have been thoughtful. Yet all this fine work may nevertheless be futile because it did not find its place in an effective process of consultation.

CONSULTATION

Organizational strategies alone cannot solve problems brought on by the inadequacies of a process. Yet, some reflection on what is involved in consultation will show that attending to organizational issues can make a contribution. To consult about a matter is to consider advice about it before deciding how to act. This means, first, that the deciding administrator has available the views of the "consultant" person or group on the issue to be decided, either because those opinions are solicited or proffered. Second, a person or group is consulted, if, before making a decision, the administrator takes those consultants' views into consideration, weighing them alongside his or her own thoughts on the matter at hand. Third, it matters *whose* views are sought and attended to. Either good sense or institutional proprieties (or both) require that the opinions of one particular person or group be heeded, while attending to other people doesn't count as consulting.

A closer look at these components of consulting will reveal some aspects that are fairly hard edged and others that are fuzzy. To begin with the third component, I'm not using good sense if I consult the kid who mows my lawn about whether I should sell my stock in IBM. A faculty could care less if the president first consulted his wife and second cousin before deciding to close the Library School. Happily, *who* should be consulted is one of the more hard edged components of this process. Indeed, in an institutional setting, it can be determined with considerable clarity which groups are appropriate to consult on which issues and how these groups should be formed. Organizational strategies can actually deal with this aspect of consultation in academic institutions. Bylaws can match issues and committees with reasonable precision.

We can rather easily determine whether an administrator is or is not in possession of the views of the appropriate consultant group, but after that we move into fuzzier territory. Was the group clear what they were consulting *about?* Were the issues understood in the same way by advisor and advisee? Did the consultant group have adequate knowledge about the issue to provide informed and relevant advice? Were the views of the consultant group furnished *before* the decision was actually made, even if not yet made public.

This last query lands us in the second component, the most difficult and important one: did the administrator actually take the advice into consideration in the thought processes that led to a decision? The belief that advice is *not* being attended to frequently gives rise to the sense of futility that leads faculty members to shun participation in governance activities. Why work hard and chew up valuable time if the result has no effect on what actually happens? The question is difficult because there may be no unambiguous signs as to whether the proffered advice was or was not actually weighed.

A cynic might see no need to answer this difficult question. Whenever the action taken by an administrator is in *conformity* with the advice given, no one much cares whether the advice was in fact *considered* by the decision maker. The end eradicates concern for the means. Moreover, in the real world—as distinguished from philosophical treatises—administrators' thought processes matter not one whit; what counts is whether the administrators *appear* to pay heed to the offered advice. The *political*—rather than philosophical—requirements for consultation are then met either when an administration does what was recommended, whether or not attention was paid to the faculty recommendation, or when it seems that the advice was listened to, whether or not it was.

The cynic has a point, since numerous institutions undoubtedly get along without having their administrators go beyond fulfilling those political requirements for consultation. But for how long can this state of affairs last, given that one needs to be clever to deceive a faculty—a company of smart and suspicious people? It may even be that the easiest way to *seem* to pay heed is actually to do so.

The cynic's responses miss what is essential. Where only the political requirements for consultation are fulfilled, collaborative decision making has not taken place at all. Yet there are good grounds for having faculty join with administrators in governing academic institutions. The different skills and funds of knowledge of these dissimilar constituencies, as well as their distinct perspectives, roles, and responsibilities, are all needed if the complex academic enterprise is to be well guided. Our goal in this book is to see what organizational characteristics may be of help in fostering actual collaborative decision making, with special concern for the key issue of faculty participation in the governance process.

INSTITUTIONAL SIZE

In considering just what kind of all-campus organization is appropriate, we note that size matters if a particular body is to be both capable of speaking for the entire institution and of functioning as a deliberative body. To begin with smaller schools, a faculty of up to about 300 members is still capable of conducting significant business as a body. Given the attendance one can reasonably expect—assuming inevitable absences from campus and a proportion of incurably uninterested—a body of this size would not be too large to be effective, when meetings were attended by more than the normally faithful. The alternative is far less desirable. If a faculty of up to 300 members delegated its authority to a council or steering committee, the relative closeness in size between the decision makers and those left out of the governance process would inevitably lead the latter to feel disenfranchised and withdraw into apathy or become chronic critics.

These observations would also apply to the faculty of a school within a university composed of several schools. At such an institution, the term "senate" would no doubt be preempted by the all-university organization. The business of a constituent school would be conducted by its faculty—perhaps simply *called* "The Faculty"—which would meet as the governing body of the school.

Although the extent of student and staff representation is difficult to discuss without taking into consideration the particular nature and history of an institution, leading members of the administration must be a part of any overall governing body. Moreover, the president (or, alternatively, the school dean) is the most appropriate officer to be in the chair. Such administrative participation is imperative to deal with the fuzzier components of consultation. No formal schemes will determine their presence, if one rules out legalistic and cumbersome devices that would make the cure worse than the disease. Administration and faculty must discuss the same issue and possess the same information that bears on it.

Initially, all relevant information is undoubtedly not shared; the administration is likely to be in possession of considerably more knowledge than most or all members of the faculty. The interaction provided for by the consultative process thus presents an opportunity for the administration to educate the faculty concerning facts about the institution relevant to the issue under consideration. In some cases, this pedagogic activity will need to address and deal with certain persistent beliefs, such as the existence of hidden sources of money that might be used to solve a problem or achieve a desirable goal if only the administration, for benign or malevolent reasons, did not refuse to deploy these sources. Ongoing interactions in a consultative process may be the only way in which suppositions of this kind can be dispelled.

The central question is how responsive relevant administrators are to faculty recommendations. Extensive regular interactions between administration and faculty will put these crucial aspects of consultation into much sharper focus. Credibility is a function of trust and, in this context, trust is gained or lost through recurring face-to-face exchanges on a variety of topics—to the point where, for better or for worse, the interlocutors come to know each others' minds. An organizational contribution can thus provide some of the conditions for making this collaboration effective, though, as ever, it takes actual human beings to make use of them.

The important point is that the senate be a working body, where the topics taken up are common *business* and discussions are likely to conclude in *actions* of some kind. But preserving the prospect of participation in considerably larger schools is much more problematic. There are two types of cases with similar obstacles. The first case concerns the global body of institutions that are like those so far discussed, but larger—either institutions that are not divided into distinctly separate schools or one large school within a university of many schools. The second pertains to the all-institution governance body of large complex universities, composed of numerous distinct colleges and schools.

In neither case is it likely that a senate composed of all faculty members—plus representation from other constituencies—will be effective in collaborative decision making in behalf of the entire institution. Were a sizeable proportion of a large faculty actually to participate in the affairs of such a senate, it would be unwieldy as a working group for doing the institution's business. If, as is much more probable, the level of participation is low—in absolute terms, as well as in the ratio of participants to those eligible—the institution's government is made vulnerable to politicking and manipulation. This dilemma effectively dictates that the role of a large senate be reduced to the primarily ceremonial. While it might actually exercise its rights as *demos* in cases of extraordinary stress, its normal functioning would be confined to once-a-term meetings for the sake of communication and to symbolize the oneness of the institution. In such cases, the work of participating in decision making in behalf of the entire institution is delegated to two dozen or so members of a senate (or faculty council), elected by the faculty at large.

Sheer size has an adverse effect on collaborative decision making. By virtue of having the conduct of joint faculty and administration business limited to delegates, the opportunity to build the kind of credibility needed to make consultation work is much reduced. Indeed, an additional credibility gap can all too easily develop between council members in frequent contact with administrators and the faculty electorate they represent. Not only do far fewer faculty members actually participate in governance activities, but, just as in civil society, voter apathy may well diminish even the minimal participation associated with periodic elections. In large universities, faculty members are likely to have more significant governance roles in the schools and colleges to which they belong. But the complementary weakness of the all-institution governance body causes many such universities to resemble federations of near-autonomous states. In their case, organizational art has been less than successful in combatting those natural centrifugal forces.

The all-campus governance body, whether a senate or a representative council, must be a working body rather than a discussion club. One way of making this more likely is to have virtually all of a school's working committees be subordinate to the senate (the term I will once again use to refer to *every* form of all-campus governance organization). The senate is thus importantly involved in the formation of these committees, which also report to the senate the results of their deliberations. Only some of these committee resolutions take the form of recommendations *to* the senate, becoming the *faculty's* recommendations or actions only after the senate itself disposes of the issue. Because most committee transactions are formally communicated to the senate, that body is not only kept broadly informed about the institution's business—whether library policies or regulations pertaining to research grants—but its members are also given the opportunity to raise questions about issues not normally acted on by that body.

THE ORGANIZATION OF BUDGETING AND PLANNING

The number of committees operating under the aegis of the senate varies widely—from as few as half a dozen to more than a score—and is by no means in direct proportion to the size and complexity of the institution. Two specific examples—those concerned with educational policy and with faculty appeals and grievances—will be taken up in Chapters 6 and 7. Now, we will take a closer look at the organization of two vital functions—consideration of the institution's budget and of its plans for the future—because they paradigmatically involve collaborative decision making at the presidential level. While a small library has been written on budgeting and planning, our concern is limited to a few observations that will shed some light as to how, in these cases, collaboration should be organized.

Both the formulation of budgets and of plans are highly dependent on full and accurate information about the institution. This is widely recognized in the age of the computer. Most institutions now have the capacity to provide large amounts of data at least about those aspects of themselves that can readily be quantified. A secondary organizational consequence follows from this wealth of data: staff must be assigned to budget and planning committees to help committee members undertrained in the use of quantitative techniques to understand and manipulate institutional data.

The profusion of information about every aspect of an institution can induce committees to misconceive their function. The technocratic outlook vainly hopes that the policy to be devised is somehow already *in* the data, needing only to be cleverly compiled so as to become manifest. But, as our next maxim illustrates, one cannot derive a picture of the façade of a palace from depictions of each of its stones: *Maxim 10. The whole is both greater and less than the sum of its parts: neither an institution's budget, plan, nor aspirations can be constructed out of those of its constituent parts.* According to this maxim, neither the budget nor the future of an institution is the sum of the budgets or futures proposed by its subdivisions and units, modified, as needed, by the reality of scarcity. Because such proposals are *merely* data, an overarching perspective and objective is needed to make those parts into components of a whole.

Although these comments apply both to budgeting and to planning, there are also differences between them. Budgeting is essentially pie slicing at a table where most of the guests arrive with virtually unassailable rights to nine-tenths of what will be coming out of the kitchen. While the recipients are anything but indifferent even to small increases and decreases in allocation, the magnitude of unavoidable expenditures, together with institutional aversions to upheaval, give relatively little room for discretion to the budget makers, whether in good years or bad.

If planning were treated in the same way as budgeting, it would consist largely of looking ahead—an essentially empirical pursuit—and only very little of making adjustments—a function of policy making. This is planning in the sense in which squirrels plan for the winter, by stashing away acorns now so as to have them later. Although colleges and universities must also do what squirrels do, another kind of planning is necessary as well. There are occasions when academic institutions will need to consider adding or dropping teaching or research programs, perhaps even an entire school; there may be reasons to think about modifying substantially an institution's size—up or down—to contemplate playing musical chairs with its space, to build new buildings, or even to move somewhere else. In short, one cannot do without the kind of planning that is open to envisaging a future that is qualitatively quite *different* from the condition that results when anticipated incremental changes are superimposed on the way things now are, and which then devises steps to reach that different future.

Planning of this grand sort will help an institution anticipate and react to changes in its intellectual, economic, and social environment; to take advantage of new developments inside and outside the institution; and to be entrepreneurial or conservative, depending on its self-image. But, as the following maxim shows, to consider and do the things that have been mentioned in this and the previous paragraphs takes a special impetus and requires rising above the conventions that fetter the imagination: *Maxim 11. Committees whose mission is to perform routine and ongoing functions are ill suited for tasks that require them to move outside the framework within which they normally operate.* If, then, a planning committee existed as a standing committee, a special, *ad hoc* committee would be needed to gather the *specific* information needed to formulate a *fresh* plan for the institution's future.

In any case, planning of the kind that can potentially change the direction of an institution is most certainly not an ongoing task. No one needs annual upheavals. Whether such a searching look is taken at regular intervals—every five or seven years—or simply whenever the campus leadership perceives the need to do so, *different* people must be harnessed to the task—fresh troops who are free of scars from previous planning battles and who bring new ideas into the fray. The kind of planning we have been talking about intermittently requires a special committee, not a standing committee.

Yet, colleges and universities must do what squirrels do, and on an ongoing basis. Institutions must look ahead, to limit the source of surprises—and consequent shocks—to external events that could *not* have been foreseen. The most effective approach to this task is precisely through the budget. The largest part of the job is empirical: predicting income and expenditures and adjusting allocations in the light of changes desired for the immediate future. Thus, the budget committee needs to perform a limited planning function. It must not only deliberate on the budget of the upcoming fiscal year, but it must project, with increasing tentativeness, a budget for each of the two subsequent years as well. If a plan of the grander sort had been adopted by the institution, the changes it calls for can in this way be incorporated, one year at a time, into the operations of the institution.

More generally, however, only where a procedure is followed that has everyone who participates in making decisions about the *present* do so in cognizance of an envisaged *future* state does planning actually make a difference to an institution. Without such meshing into the operations of a college or university, planning would merely be an epiphenomenal activity. In violation of *Maxim 2*, much time would be lavished on a labor and strife intensive activity that remains unjustified because it fails to serve an institutional purpose.

[2] Some means cannot be justified by any end; nevertheless, the only way in which a means can be justified at all is by showing that it contributes to bringing about a desired end.

SOME PRINCIPLES OF COMMITTEE FORMATION

Budgeting and planning are sufficiently important central functions to deserve express attention. But short of creating an unreadable compendium, we cannot consider all types of committees that might appropriately be created in a college or university. Instead, let us take up some principles of committee formation aimed at making them more effective at the business of collaborative decision making. But what justifies the existence of a committee in the first place? To justify its existence, a *standing* committee must have *ongoing* tasks to perform. If something needs tending, by all means, minister to it; but good government is undermined by the wastefulness of committees that have little of substance to do—if only because meetings devoted to unnecessarily concocted busy work breed cynicism.

The formation of *ad hoc* or *special* committees to accomplish one-time or infrequently recurring tasks makes more economical use of an institution's human capital, such can be constituted with the specific job in mind. Finally, such intermittent and unpredictable needs as the resolution of grievances are best met by the creation of *panels* whose members are called upon to act only when and if. Admittedly, it is not always obvious what is an ongoing and what is a sporadic task. When in doubt, abstain from the creation of a standing committee, recalling the requirement of *Maxim 2* that means be justified by one of the institution's goals.

[2] Some means cannot be justified by any end; nevertheless, the only way in which a means can be justified at all is by showing that it contributes to bringing about a desired end.

Further, there is the question of the individuation of committees. Many ongoing tasks need to be performed on campuses; when should some bundle of tasks be assigned to a single committee, and when to two committees? Mostly, the answer is obvious, but at times it is not; e.g., should admissions and financial aid be one committee or two? One rule of thumb recommends the creation of two separate committees only where each group can accomplish the mission assigned to it without significant overlap in work done with the other group, and when there is no undue risk that one committee will make recommendations that are signigicantly incompatible with those of the other committee.

But even where there is significant overlap, there may still be reasons to have different people work on different, though related, tasks. For such cases, a much underused device recommends itself. Let there *be* two (or more) committees, but have one be the *sub*committee of the other, or even one of several subcommittees of a parent committee. While the work of a budget committee and a benefits committee, for example, call for different perspectives and skills, they can nevertheless not function effectively without close communication with each other—

two facts that suggest the latter should be a subcommittee of the former. Finally, it may often not be so clear whether two separate committees are appropriate or not. In such cases of doubt, bring to mind *Maxim 1* and strike a blow in the battle against centrifugality by refraining from creating separate committees.

[1] *In academic institutions, the forces of* nature *are centrifugal; organizational* art *must be used to create propensities toward coherence.*

We turn next to the composition of committees in academic institutions: Who should be on a committee? How should the members get on committees? What should be the size of a committee and the terms of service of members? Senate committees must be "mixed" and include, in addition to faculty members, the administrator responsible for the domain of a particular committee and, where appropriate, representation from staff or students. Collaboration requires that all parties are in possession of the information relevant to a given issue and that they have a high degree of understanding of the viewpoints of different constituencies, even of the motives that underlie those opinions. The first of these conditions is difficult to achieve without ongoing interaction, and the second is well nigh impossible, especially without the kind of familiarity necessary for credibility.

Purists at times object to such mingling and insist that faculty members should, by themselves, arrive at an unalloyed *faculty* position before presenting it to the administration. Such objectors, however, are pure about the wrong thing. Tacit in their position seems to be an appeal to Montesquieuean checks and balances, a view that requires one to think of the faculty as the legislature and the administration as the executive branch. That governmental analogy, however, does not withstand scrutiny, any more than does that of the corporation. Accordingly, rather than borrowing devices from inappropriate models, the goal of effective institutional decision making must be kept at the center of the inquiry, with systematic interaction of faculty and administration serving as a means to that end.

Still, committees are mostly composed of faculty members. How should they be selected for service? The following maxim helps answer that question: *Maxim 12. Choosing the members of a committee in a way appropriate to its function is likely to increase the effectiveness of its operation.* But some reflection on the purposes of committees reveals a complication. The name of a committee usually suggests what the medievals would call its *terminus ad quem*, the tasks it is meant to accomplish: formulate a budget, make educational policy, or oversee intercollegiate athletics. But tacitly or explicitly, committee members have one or more of three additional functions of a different sort, the kind those scholastics would call a *terminus a quo*. This second set of functions is most relevant to the question of how persons come to be committee members.

First, the job of committee members is often to speak and act in behalf of a certain set of interests. Their role is to *represent*—sometimes a group of people (staff, untenured faculty, graduating seniors), sometimes of a specific enterprise (graduate education, laboratory research, computer use). As in the larger political world, the appropriate way to select committee members as *representatives* is to have them elected by those they represent. The constituency-electors are often obvious: all members of the staff, or every untenured faculty member (for committees concerned with their welfare). Sometimes the purpose must be formulated more specifically, if the electorate is to be properly identified. Thus, a committee that is to determine details about *upcoming* graduation festivities takes up an interest only of *this* year's graduating seniors. One charged with making changes in placement policies deals with concerns of *future* graduating seniors, a fact that suggests that all future seniors who are now at the institution are entitled to be represented. At other times it will be known who should be represented only if more than the usual clarity is achieved about a committee's mission. Who should be represented might be answered one way, for example, if a committee's job were the nuts-and-bolts regulation of graduate education and in another way if its mandate were the consideration of the place of graduate education among the other enterprises of the institution. It makes a difference whether a parking committee's job is to see how those who park on campus are best served or whether it is to consider the interests both of those who park and those who don't.

The responsibility of some committees or panels—their *terminus ad quem*—is juridical. Someone must listen to appeals from adverse decisions, to grievances stemming from a variety of contexts, and deal with breaches of regulations, most frequently on the part of students. *Being fair* is the vital secondary function of those engaged in adjudication. Without a widely held belief that these judicial roles are performed equitably, an institution is better off with purely administrative justice. The procedures used matter, and so does the conscientiousness with which they are followed, topics to which we return in Chapter 7. Nearly as important is the way in which the adjudicators are selected. Deeply ingrained in our common law tradition is the requirement that we be judged by our peers and that those peers are chosen, for any given case, in a way that does not antecedently make one outcome more likely than another. Accordingly, panels from which adjudicators are selected for particular cases might be elected by (and only by) the peers liable to be subject to their judgments, or they might be chosen by lot from the roster of peers. For the sake of fairness, a particular case could be handled by a group of peers randomly selected from the appropriate panel, modified by a method for disqualifying those who have an antecedent interest in the case.

The *terminus ad quem* of a third type of committee calls for some special expertise on the part of its members or at least a distinct interest in and experience with a specific set of issues. Some instances are obvious: a committee that overseas an electron microscopy facility should be composed of members who are knowledgeable about those instruments. Other instances call for common sense and are therefore more controversial. A committee on computer use should not be limited to computer specialists, any more than a committee on undergraduate education should consist of alleged experts on that topic. But, the first of these groups would not be well served by members who haven't used computers and don't intend to, nor the second by faculty members who have never stood in a classroom with undergraduates. Finally, some cases involve disagreement and debate, such as whether budget making or planning requires broad experience or long association with the institution—an issue that is often resolved by calling for a committee membership that includes all ranks.

If expertise were the only secondary requirement for membership on a committee, the most efficacious way of putting together a committee would be simply to appoint it, with advice from those who know who the relevant specialists are. But because often those experts also need to *represent* some constituency—and because people don't take kindly to having their representatives appointed—the need for special experience is frequently sacrificed. Members are elected, accompanied by the hope, repeatedly disappointed, that voters and candidates have the sense to pay heed to the need for special competence. Yet, there are ways of having your cake and eating it too. One is to make use of a group—call it a committee on committees or a nominating committee, ideally including an informed administrator—to prepare a slate of candidates who possess the requisite experience from among the constituencies to be represented. Where expertise is required by an adjudicative panel— as in the consideration of a charge of scientific misconduct—it is appropriate for nominators to develop an inclusive roster of peers who are qualified and then to use some random method to select the members. In this way, the need for special knowledge minimizes any compromise with fairness.

Next, we turn to a brief consideration of the size of committees. Assuming some minimum number—as related to the purpose of the committee—the following maxim sums up most everything else that needs to be said: *Maxim 13. As a committee increases in size, its capacity to be representative becomes greater, while its potentiality for effectiveness decreases.* College and university committees have a tendency to become unwieldy as a result of the desire to represent everyone who might have a claim to be represented. Since one reason for such meticulousness is to increase the likelihood of broad acceptance of the outcome of the committee's deliberations, it will help to keep *Maxim 13* in mind, together with the fact that the *quality* of a committee's work also has a bearing on its acceptance.

Finally, as to the terms of committee members, a standing committee should be organized with staggered terms, usually three years in duration. In this way, a committee can change with the inevitable changes in the institution and yet benefit in obvious ways from the possession of a memory. Moreover, as the following maxim explains, there is much merit to limiting the number of consecutive terms a faculty member may serve: *Maxim 14. The longer committee members represent a constituency, the more they tend to be drawn away from the faculty members and activities to be represented.* A cadre of academic politicians is spawned where this paradox of representation is ignored. At its worst, college or university business is reduced to mere campus politics, with the politicians out of touch and lacking credibility as the faculty's agents. What is intended to be joint decision making is, in fact, not. If only to accord with *Maxim 9*, this vicious circle must be avoided.

[9] *The number and quality of persons who participate in governance activities are directly related to how effectively they influence conditions that matter to them.*

CHAPTER 3

Primary Academic Administration: The Office of the Dean of a School

THE FUNCTIONS OF THE OFFICE OF THE DEAN OF A SCHOOL

I have been insisting, perhaps superfluously, that the academic enterprise is the cardinal function of the institutions this book is concerned with. This enterprise involves teaching and learning in all of its aspects, the conduct of research, and the pursuit of other creative activities. We now begin a sequence of three chapters devoted to the administration of this central endeavor, ever mindful of *Maxim 2*, which tells us that academic administrators and their offices and activities must be justifiable as serving and fostering that many-sided undertaking.

[2] Some means cannot be justified by any end; nevertheless, the only way in which a means can be justified at all is by showing that it contributes to bringing about a desired end.

We begin in this chapter with what I call primary academic administration, the locus, for example, of much of the specific decision making about the composition and deployment of the faculty. Most often the responsible officer is the dean of a school or college, while in some colleges, the primary overseer of the academic enterprise is called the dean of the faculty or even vice president or provost. But in most universities and in many colleges this *primary* academic administrator is not the *chief* academic administrator, there being an organizational level to which deans and other unit heads report. Chapter 4, accordingly, is devoted to that office. Finally, many schools or colleges are segmented into departments or programs, an organizational level taken up in Chapter 6. Throughout these discussions, we will want to relate organizational scheme to administrative mission, but, especially, to become clear about the differences in roles of these organizational levels.

Three broad functions can be singled out as lying at the center of the primary academic officer's role: the administration of the school's curricula, the overseeing of guidance for the schools students, and the maintenance of the school's faculty. We start our discussion with the last of these jobs, because it dominates the work of a dean—first, because faculty members are the agents who carry out the school's teaching, advising, and research; and second, because so much of the time and effort of a dean's office is devoted to the care and feeding of the faculty.

Faculty maintenance begins with the allocation of positions of different kinds and continues with the overseeing of the recruitment that fills them, the assignment of salaries and raises, and the administration of the process that leads to the renewal of an appointment, a promotion, or a dismissal. Irregular personnel functions consume almost as much of the dean's time: dealing with every kind of request, complaint, and transgression; adjudicating disagreements; handling outside offers; coping in numerous ways with large yet tender egos; and much more. Further, the members of the faculty need to be supported in their teaching and research, with the dean playing a crucial role in the allocation of staff personnel, leaves or sabbaticals, facilities, and equipment. Finally, a dean must select (and persuade) faculty members to do the institution's business as departmental chairpersons or committee members and he or she must interact in various ways with faculty departments, programs, and committees.

Although *Maxim 3* states that academic administrators do not simply *manage* units of faculty, there is a management as well as a leadership component in most of a dean's functions. Although an oversimplification, we can again understand the first of these activities as concerned with the means end of the continuum and the second as addressing goals. What stands out in this context, however, is that so much of management consists of the application of rules, procedures, and policies, especially those concerned with personnel and budget decisions. Some of these rules are

[3] *Academic administrators do not manage units composed of faculty or students, however much they may at times dream of doing so.*

of the dean's own devising, many stem from "higher" levels. Much of the dean's work comes to him or her in the form of requests and proposals, from departments, programs, committees, and individual faculty members. Interspersed occasionally is something stronger than a request emanating from a superior.

It clearly makes a difference how a dean responds to these service station duties—more or less within established rules, policies, and trajectories, more or less creatively—so that even as reagent a dean may be wholly managerial or exercise considerable leadership. Finally, a dean may act as initiator of changes and projects and not simply in response to requests. As such, a dean is more clearly cast in the role of leader, though deanish originality is not the issue. Posited changes and projects will seldom emerge full blown from the dean's head, but will more likely be distillates of interactions with faculty members, students, and others. And so much the better, since the needs of leadership are served to the degree to which there are followers, making deanly initiating much more apt to succeed where impulses in the proposed direction are already represented in the community.

THE ORGANIZATION OF THE OFFICE
Administration of the Faculty

Where an institution is small enough for a dean to know all the school's faculty reasonably well and to meet regularly with the chairpersons of departments and programs, no deep structural issues about the dean's office are raised. In such circumstances, a "hands on" dean can interview all faculty candidates who come to campus, personally consider all faculty requests above the trivial, and steer the programmatic directions of the school through interactions with individuals and committees. With the aid of a couple of assistants, including one who has the skills of an accountant, such deans are likely to do as good a job as their abilities and bosses let them. The structure of the dean's office does, however, become an issue above a certain threshold of school size or complexity. Although that level will also vary with a dean's appetite for work, it is most certainly reached when a dean has no time left to think or to initiate projects of his or her own.

For an enlarged dean's office, the implications of the management-leadership distinction once more move into the foreground. We have observed that a significant part of the work of a dean consists of tasks, including important ones, that are governed by an abundance of policies and rules, including, but not limited to, the implementation of procedures that originated in the dean's office. In the administration of these processes—many of them concerned with decisions about personnel and the allocation of resources—it certainly matters whether the job is done well or poorly. Nevertheless, a good portion of this management function is routine and consists of applying—or overseeing the application of—general rules to particular cases.

What is routine can be routinized, suggesting a model in which assistants become versed in various processes and sets of regulations, applying them to the material that comes into the office. On such a scheme, their task is to move along what is in conformity, seek correction for what is correctable, and deny what fails to pass muster. Whatever sonorous titles might be possessed by such masters-of-procedures, they are in effect staff assistants because little if any authority is delegated to them. Discretion—and therefore real decision power—is left to the dean, who might be thought of as sitting at the center of a hive of worker bees.

More likely at the hub of a bureaucracy! In the model just sketched, assistants, by whatever name, are inevitably judged to be successful to the degree to which they keep the office running smoothly and out of trouble with "higher" powers. The predominant motives easily become negative: to *prevent* mistakes and to *refrain* from adding to the dean's burden by calling on that officer's discretionary authority. For functionaries who are essentially keepers of certain procedures, no significant accomplishments are envisaged that are extrinsic to the processes in their charge. Reflection on a scheme that sharply divides the routine from discretionary authority yields the following important maxim with relevance to the organization of a dean's office and beyond: *Maxim 15. An office that lacks goals of its own will tend to give priority to getting the process right over getting the job done.*

But work needs to get done and how faculty are recruited and compensated matters. Deans *do* need assistance in the supervision of those processes, but not in this way. Judgment—discretion—is called for more often than one might think, if only because of the number of variables usually involved, the imprecision with which they can be measured, and the unavoidable amateurishness of faculty members engaged in administrative activity. And the exercise of discretion is inevitably contextual. A dean determines which way to lean, how much to lean, or whether to lean at all, in the light of overall academic goals, on the one hand, and of information gathered in the course of numerous interactions with faculty members, departments, and chairpersons, on the other. *Maxim 8* reminds us that most decisions have budgetary implications, and if we recognize that times of budgetary stringency are normal rather than the exception, the larger portion of a dean's constituency may in some way be affected by the handling of a

[8] Few significant campus decisions are without budgetary implications.

specific case. Moreover, just as the same fund of money cannot be appropriated twice, the allocation of space demonstrates even more eloquently the finitude of the world we live in.

This leaves us with assistants reporting on the degree of the congruity of recommendations with the policies and regulations that pertain to them and the dean making all the decisions. We are where we were, with no help proffered for the school too large to be run by a dean with just a couple of assistants. We must try another model, one that does not presuppose a sharp distinction between the routine and the discretionary.

Needed are dean's helpers who, because conversant with the academic enterprise of the school, are capable of exercising discretionary authority, but who nevertheless remain subordinate to the dean, rather than develop fiefdoms of their own. While the tensions among these requirements are of the sort that prompted Mao to foment his bloody Cultural Revolution, more peaceful strategies should be available in the academy. First, both for the sake of their capability and their credibility, these associate deans (to give these administrators a title) must be persons who might actually become deans; they must be respected faculty members. But there is a need to diminish the likelihood that their subordinate status will induce such associates to engage in bureaucratic role aggrandizement, given the warning of *Maxim 15* that manner, instead of substance, can become the goal. Therefore, these positions should be rotating, with a maximum service of two three-year terms, and their holders should actually be rotated, as advocated by the maxim that follows: *Maxim 16. Where*

[15] An office that lacks goals of its own will tend to give priority to getting the process right over getting the job done.

administrators who hold rotating positions are not actually rotated, reality overtakes intent. Finally, if only to enable such associate deans to retain viability as faculty members, their deanly duties should be less than full time, allowing them to continue with some teaching or research activity.

The size and complexity of the school—as well as the extra-academic demands on the dean (see below)—will determine the number of associate deans to be brought into the office. One aspect of their complex role is to become familiar with an agreed-upon segment of the school—typically, a group of departments or programs—by serving as an interface between that constituency and the dean's office. This means interacting with faculty members, committees, and chairpersons in ways the dean would. A second aspect of an associate dean's role is to be an ongoing counselor to the dean, both by informing that officer of the issues and problems existing in his or her assigned domain, and by assisting in the formulation of directions and policies for the entire school and in decisions about allocations of faculty positions, funds, space, etc.

Given extensive intra-office communication of this kind and with an agreed-upon dean's office strategy, an area of discretionary action can be carved out for an associate dean. With working relationships what they should be, there is no need for a codification of which decisions fall within the sphere entrusted to the judgment of an associate dean and which must be taken to the dean for disposition. Thus, the determination of "normal" salary increases, for example, may well be left to such an associate dean—working within a framework of more global allocations and salary policies—while making special efforts in response to outside offers are appropriately handled or supervised by the dean.

How should the components of a school be parcelled out to associate deans? Although the following principles are appropriate to schools of every kind, our specific concern now is with colleges of arts and sciences. The thesis to be propounded is that one must resist the understandable temptation to assign the natural sciences to one person, the social sciences to a second, and the humanities to a third. Instead, each associate dean's portfolio should contain sample departments from *each* of the traditional divisions.

Two different kinds of consideration support this proposal. First, so as to have associate deans serve effectively as a group of dean's advisors, each member should be familiar with all aspects of the school. Budgetary issues, to take a single but prominent example, differ sharply from each other in such departments as chemistry, economics, and classical languages. All counselors should not only know, but understand this and have a feel for the differences. Second, divisional representation inevitably creates divisional spokespersons. Having advocates for different types of study vie with each other for the dean's largesse is not constructive. If there is to be rivalry among departments, let it be on the grounds of their excellence, on the importance of their subject to a liberal education, on the quality of their teaching, or even about their usefulness to the job market or their popularity with students. Some benefit might spring from such contests. But there is neither educational nor other institutional merit to competition along the lines of the traditional divisions, e.g., sciences *versus* the humanities *versus* social sciences.

If it is inadvisable to parcel out departments to associate deans in conformity with the traditional divisions of study, it is even less advisable to elevate these divisions to the status of schools. Size tends to be a determinative reason for devising a scheme that creates a school each for the natural sciences, the social sciences, and the humanities—with some of them further subdivided. The convenience of having birds of a feather flock together is another ground for such a development, though most such subdivisions are still likely to house a few departments that do not quite fit.

But if expediency justifies this administrative device, we are nevertheless confronting means that bring about educationally undesirable consequences. The following maxim applies in the academy even more than in the larger world: *Maxim 17. Boundaries are less likely to create solidarity among those who live within them than they constitute barriers for those residing outside them.* The heaviest price for these divisions is paid by undergraduate students, since far more of them are destined to become foreigners rather than citizens of these realms. Each school develops curricula, procedures, and attitudes for "our" students—that is, for majors in its disciplines. A second package is devised for those who are merely "their" students—that is, majors in disciplines resident in other schools. It is all too likely, that for "them," the science, social science, and humanities courses that are made available are dutiful at their best and more probably downright condescending. And where there is no institutional pressure, not much of any sort is offered to outsiders—on the model of universities with music schools, at which arts and science students have less opportunity to study music than in the smallest and poorest liberal arts colleges in the country. Students, accordingly, do not by any means have equal access to all parts of the world of knowledge, with the differences not determined by interest and affinity, but by bureaucratically devised citizenship papers.

Graduate students essentially live within their particular departments, a fact that in any case reduces the benefit for them of working in a school made up of related departments. But at least half of the instruction of undergraduates comes from outside their major department and often substantially more than that; to reduce the conception of an undergraduate simply to that of major in a certain subject is to slight a substantial and important part of such a student's education. What could be more appropriate, in an educational institution, than to have the administrative art called for in *Maxim 1* work to overcome centrifugality in behalf of its *students*?

[1] *In academic institutions, the forces of* nature *are centrifugal; organizational* art *must be used to create propensities toward coherence.*

I do not expect this little sermon to persuade many university administrators to try to reconstitute a school of arts and sciences from the several pieces into which it has long since disintegrated. Yet I do hope that institutions where this has not yet happened will consider seeking alternative ways of coping with size than in this traditional but misguided way.

Ministering to Students

This entire chapter, so far, has been devoted to the administration of the faculty; it is time we turned to the primary academic administrator's responsibility vis-a-vis students. Graduate students obtain their advice and guidance from the departments in which they are studying, supervised, with a light hand, by a graduate dean. But if only because undergraduates and professional students are not wholly assignable to departments—or not at all—the responsibility for their guidance and disciplining must be assumed at a higher level. *Maxim 4* reminds us that the way a job is performed is affected by the kind of supervision the performer receives. This alone is sufficient for recommending that the person administering the system of advising and disciplining be an associate dean who reports directly to the primary academic head of the school—to make it more likely that students' encounters with that system are informed by the academic goals and values of the institution.

[4] *To what position a given officer reports significantly affects the way in which his or her responsibilities are discharged.*

A second reason is more specific. One of the functions of primary academic administration is the care of the (undergraduate or professional) curriculum. Even in periods in which no fundamental reforms are contemplated or called for, there is an abiding need to make adjustments in the face of ever-changing conditions, a need to coordinate offerings and to assure the maintenance of their quality, as well as to support in various ways the "delivery" of the school's curriculum, that is, the teaching of the faculty. When these steady state issues are taken up, they must be rooted in empirical knowledge about the students being educated and not solely considered in the light of educational theory and ideology. It is appropriate, therefore, that the administrator who acts for the dean by taking a leading role in the management of the curriculum be the same associate dean who oversees the advising of students.

In contrast to this recommended scheme, an institution-wide deanship for undergraduate studies is at times proposed or created. The aim need not be the (probably) vain one of achieving greater efficiency. The intent may be, instead, the laudable one of giving recognition to the importance of such student-related functions by raising the status of the person who oversees undergraduate studies to the same level as school deans, rather than leaving the several schools to deal with these concerns. Yet, while perhaps promoting the *visibility* of undergraduate education, such a scheme is unlikely to make for effective *advocacy*. *Maxim 8* applies with a vengeance: curricular decisions have budgetary implications. And since the character of the curriculum ultimately rests on the makeup of the faculty, the achievement of an undergraduate dean's curricular goals require both a budget and authority approximating those of a primary academic administrator.

[8] *Few significant campus decisions are without budgetary implications.*

Giving similar powers to two different officers is not workable, whether each is expected to act alone or whether they are meant somehow to collaborate. Therefore, the creation of an independent undergraduate deanship violates the following important principle: *Maxim 18. The responsibilities of an office must not exceed its authority, including budgetary authority.* The visibility of a central office of undergraduate education, is likely to arouse expectations in the campus community that its incumbent cannot fulfill. The result may well be widespread frustration and even cynicism, and it will almost surely violate *Maxim 2* by maintaining an administrative office that does not really serve a purpose.

[2] *Some means cannot be justified by any end; nevertheless, the only way in which a means can be justified at all is by showing that it contributes to bringing about a desired end.*

The scheme proposed here does not, of course, guarantee that undergraduate education will be well served and that a sufficient portion of a dean's budget will be dedicated to its support. But the designation of an associate dean to deal with curriculum and advising does assign responsibility with some clarity. In effect, it appoints the dean to the role of the faculty's executive officer for the curriculum and its delivery, even though this primary academic administrator delegates to an associate most of the operations pertaining

[4] To what position a given officer reports significantly affects the way in which his or her responsibilities are discharged.

to that function. Ultimate reliance is once again placed on the workings of *Maxim 4*: the task of the person to whom the dean reports—provost or president—is to make sure that adequate attention and support are given to undergraduate or professional education.

THE ORGANIZATION OF SUPPORT AND EXTRA-ACADEMIC ACTIVITIES

There was a time when this chapter would now have been concluded— all dean's office functions and staff at least touched upon. Today, such a purely academic deanery is no longer the norm, and is perhaps found only among a proportion of liberal arts colleges and among smaller single-purpose institutions such as certain free standing theological seminaries. We are speaking of different kinds of support staff. The assistant who can count may have grown into a full-fledged budget officer, perhaps with several subordinates of his or her own. An assistant or associate conversant with the physical underpinnings of teaching and research may have developed into a full time aide for facilities and equipment. A dean or associate dean experienced enough to be helpful to departments in solving problems with secretarial or laboratory staff might have become the school's personnel officer. Such aides play the role of specialized staff assistants, analogous to those attached to presidential offices. Although often endowed with considerable knowledge and experience, they do not control a domain of their own, but serve the needs of dean and associate deans, on the one hand, and the departments and faculty of the school, on the other.

But that is not the full story. These specialist positions materialize in deans' offices when an institution becomes too complex and large for the central service organization to minister to particular units in a satisfactory way. In principle, the central establishments could be augmented by staff persons especially designated to deal with the budgetary, facilities, or personnel needs of particular schools, though there are at least two reasons why this tends not to happen. First, the *need* to have such positions created comes into being long before central administration officers can be persuaded of that fact. As Goethe's Faust asserts, in the beginning was the deed (and not a new budget slot). Second, central budget, plant, or human resources offices are organized by different *specialties*: into such schemes it is awkward to fit staff persons whose functions are defined as working to support particular *schools*. But there is an overriding reason why it is highly *preferable* to have this work done by staff persons housed in the schools themselves. What is needed and how it should be done is not only a function of the requirements, mores, and even idiosyncrasies of a given college or school, but of the particular individuals who constitute it at a specific time and of the particular goals its leadership just then aims to accomplish. This kind of specificity can only be achieved by someone working closely with the people who are served and someone who is responsible to the person who administers the school.

The role of such assistants is to serve the needs of their school. The setting within which they work, however, is not confined to that school, for those central establishments for budgeting, facilities, or personnel can hardly be ignored. Indeed, incumbents of these positions must act as intermediaries between center and school, with their success in serving their school in part dependent on how well they function as go-betweens. Not only do institution-wide policies govern the would-be actions of these specialists, but in countless ways there must be cooperation and even collaboration between central administration staff and the staffs of particular schools. Accordingly, even though the reporting line of these staff members is contained unambiguously within the school, they must be selected with a view to their ability to work with their central administration counterparts.

While collaboration with central units is in practice needed for specialists whose concerns are internal to the institution, they are in principle required for those engaged in external affairs. The same schools or colleges—most of them embedded in universities—that have at least some of the personnel just discussed are likely to have reached the point at which they house their own development and alumni affairs officer. The reason for this evolution, if not identical to the story just told, is at least analogous. Increasing pressure during recent decades to raise funds from private sources has led to the realization that the willingness to give is at times correlated with potential donors' affinity with and loyalty to the institutions to which they are likely to contribute. Therefore, cultivating donors at the level of component schools is advisable, including and especially, the alumni of those schools, who should be cultivated by people *within* the schools because they are more familiar with the donors and potentially closer to them. For the schools, the advisable is of course profitable, since successes in school development efforts constitute additions to the budgets of those schools. Furthermore, development officers reporting to the head of a school will become familiar with its values and sensitive to its priorities and work with the dean and other staff members in ways that are analogous to the collaboration of development head and president. Given skill and luck, the funding of a school development officer is beneficial to the school.

Central establishments for development and alumni relations need not regard such school efforts as interference, since the advent of segmentation in fund raising shows that practice is not a single-sum game. What is gained by a school need not be a loss for the university, since there is no assurance that benefactions not received by a school would have gone to the university. But a powerful "other things being equal" is in operation here. Alumni of schools are also alumni of the university. No infallible signs reveal whether potential donors are likely to be more generous to a school or the university. And surely, everyone engaged in fund raising will want as "targets" all those persons whose profiles suggest that they are in a position to make substantial contributions.

There is a dire need, therefore, to keep acrimony out of the inevitable squabbles over potential donors with multiple institutional affiliations. Moreover, nothing undermines the effectiveness of fund raising so much as an absence of coordination that has some potential donors approached by more than one agency within an institution and others not at all. Institution-wide development endeavors must be organized in ways to prevent conflict or competition with school efforts. The latter must be seen as parts of the larger whole. Such a goal is difficult to achieve, but a necessary condition for its attainment is that all the institution's development projects are subject to the same discipline. This means a particular school's development officer must report to the person who directs the fund raising division for the entire institution.

For better or for worse, we have reached a conclusion that is surely contrary to good organizational practice: the establishment of an office in which the incumbent must not only serve as a mediator between two offices, but actually stand in a reporting relationship to two officers whose interests and directives can conflict. The unavoidability of this predicament is then mitigated only by the cooperation of the two bosses in question. Dean and development vice president (or surrogate) must collaborate in the *selection* of the school development officer and must join in that person's periodic *evaluation*. Finally—and of equal importance—they must communicate with each other *directly* to avoid setting an impossible task for their subordinate: the resolution of conflicts between his or her superiors.

By no means have all possible members of school deans' offices been mentioned or discussed. But I hope that a full range of the *types* of positions to be found there has been taken up. Moreover, the hybrid dean's office roles considered in this concluding section should also be regarded as examples of positions found in other parts of many campuses. While no formula will guarantee the successful realization, full awareness of their special character of these roles is necessary.

While this discussion brings to a close our consideration of the office of a school dean, it does not end the discussion of academic administration, for we turn next to the role of chief academic officer. Because two offices are engaged in overseeing the academic enterprise, we must try to understand clearly the differences in functions between dean and provost.

CHAPTER 4

The Office of the Provost, the Chief Academic Officer

THE REALM OF THE PROVOST: AN OVERVIEW

A n administrative office is needed between the level of dean and president wherever an institution exceeds a certain complexity. To understand how this office of academic vice president or provost (I favor the shorter term) might be effectively organized, we need to know its main functions and how it differs from the dean's office, that is, from primary academic administration. We begin, however, with a vital provostial function that does not so much bear on the structure of the provost's own office as on its relationship to others, especially that of the president.

Where the office exists, the provost is the institution's highest academic administrator; where it does not, these preliminary comments apply to the dean of the faculty as chief academic officer. This role makes the provost into the college's or university's principal spokesperson for the academic enterprise. Deans of various schools must interpret and champion the ventures of their own units to a variety of audiences, but the provost is the primary proponent of the totality of the institution's academic functions. As such, the provost's first responsibility is to serve as advocate within the institution—to the president and the presidential staff, as well as to the board of trustees—and to a variety of outside constituencies. Where the voice of the highest academic officer is not persistently audible, the centrality of the scholarly and pedagogic missions is readily obscured by a babble of competing claims, especially in large and multi-partite organizations. To serve as an effective proponent, therefore, a provost must have *de facto* access to the head of the institution on an ongoing basis, well beyond the formal reporting relationship expressed by a table of organization.

The number of persons who might report to the chief academic officer can be formidable. Although many of these will be mentioned here, if only to give a sense of the potential scope of the officers a provost might be called upon to supervise, most will be taken up in more detail in the next chapter, where attention can be given to alternative reporting lines for various positions. There, too, special heed will be paid to the case of a dean of the faculty, who serves both as primary and as chief academic administrator.

The primary administrators of schools and colleges are the most obvious among those who report to the provost. In large universities, these will surely include the deans of schools of arts and sciences, business, education, engineering, fine arts, law, library science, music, social work, and more. A discussion of the organizational place of medical, dental, and other health science schools will be left for the next chapter, since the place of their executives in the list of those reporting to the provost is more controversial.

Potentially, the roster of administrators supervised by the provost continues with the heads of centers and institutes that are essentially devoted to research, wherever these are not housed within a particular school. Precisely because their interdisciplinarity places them outside school boundaries, they need special help in overcoming their isolation, as predicted by *Maxim 17*. Next are the directors of what one might call para-academic organizations that variously support the work of faculty members and students of some or all of the institution's primary academic establishments. No college or university is without a library and few are now without all-campus academic computing services. Many colleges and universities have special instrumental facilities, museums, collections of artifacts or specimen from which the denizens of more than one school benefit. A number of institutions harbor scholarly presses, establishments that often look outward to a larger world and are less connected to the faculty of the institution itself. There are *prima facie* reasons for having all of these report to the provost, although some second thoughts will be voiced in Chapter 5.

[17] Boundaries are less likely to create solidarity among those who live within them than they constitute barriers for those residing outside them.

Finally, a number of significant functions cut across school lines; those who direct these activities are candidates for reporting to the provost, albeit some of them controversially so: student affairs, graduate studies, research, and the cluster of activities performed by the office of the registrar. Potentially, then, the number of officers reporting to the chief academic officer is enormous, considerably larger than the group we considered for supervision by the president. Although mindful that this issue must be tackled—especially in light of *Maxim 5* reminding us that supervising is work—we will postpone dealing with it to the end of this chapter, so that we might first understand what a provost is supposed to do.

[5] Supervising is work, calling for the dedication of time, energy, and know-how.

THE FUNCTIONS OF THE PROVOST

Two interterrelated functions stand out as central to the provost's role as chief academic officer: the formulation of the academic goals and standards of the institution, together with the overseeing of their implementation, and the allocation of resources both to the institution's academic units and the units that support their operations. Each academic unit of an institution has its own vocation, the particular bundle of disciplines, professions, callings that are subsumed under its appellation: school of law, social work, arts and sciences, medicine, education, etc. Yet for each of them, an indefinitely large number of versions is possible—different combinations of subfields, different emphases and styles, considerable ranges in scope and size. The institution as a whole has an interest in the course chosen by its various schools since the whole is *at least* the sum of its parts. The provost's responsibility—with presidential consent and endorsement and in consultation with faculty members and other administrative officers—is to speak for this all-college or all-university academic mission.

Maxim 1 is powerfully present here. Left alone, each school will pursue its goals with little or no attention to the activities of sister schools. The *provostial* art in framing institutional goals must work against nature's centrifugality, fostering symbiotic relationships and common themes that encourage the kind of working together that makes the whole greater than the sum of its parts.

[1] In academic institutions, the forces of nature are centrifugal; organizational art must be used to create propensities toward coherence.

The need to create propensities toward coherence goes beyond the schools and colleges of an institution. Within them, tendencies to centrifugality are obvious, given that these divisions have their own subject matter, students, and constituencies beyond the institution's walls, but such tendencies prevail almost equally in units that are brought into being to support these academic divisions. For reasons we need not recount here, libraries, computer centers, offices of graduate study or of registrars have a tendency to generate goals of their own that are not necessarily congruent with the reason for their existence: to serve the needs of the faculty and students of the institution's academic units. The provost's role, as chief academic officer, is to contain these centrifugal forces as well, by working toward the integration of the work of such supporting units into the mission of the institution as a whole.

It is convenient, if superficial, to distinguish between stating goals as to *what* diverse activities are to be accomplished and formulating policies as to *how* these activities are to be accomplished. Clearly, part of a provost's task is to set institutional standards as well as to formulate and promulgate institution-wide procedures—especially with respect to academic personnel—that will help to attain these standards. This task requires consultation not only with faculty committees, as described in Chapter 2, but with the deans and directors, who are the first to have their activities affected by these provostial doings.

If this account makes provostial functions seem largely rhetorical, that might, alas, occasionally be reality. But it is hardly what is called for. Aside from *articulating* goals, *formulating* policies and standards, and *promulgating* procedures, the provost oversees their *implementation*. This administrative activity—to which the body of this chapter is devoted—is decisively reinforced by two pivotal functions. The provost possesses determinative authority both in the selection of the deans and directors of the units that report to the chief academic officer and, above all, in the allocation of resources to all units in the provostial domain. Resources means money, mostly, but also space, and access to diverse services and facilities. Indeed, where the provost serves as chief operating officer (to refer back to our earlier discussion in Chapter 1), the range of the provost's allocational authority comprises the entire institution. Where *both* provost *and* business vice president report directly to the president, the former vies with the latter for funding of the academic enterprise, the realm to which the provost's dominion is limited. While the first of the two structures gives greater prominence to the institution's academic affairs, in both of them the power to allocate support gives teeth to provostial proclamations of goals and policies.

THE ROLE OF THE PROVOST: SCYLLA AND CHARYBDIS

As we look at the functions of a chief academic officer just outlined, it is worth noting that most of them hover near the goal end of a means-end continuum, giving the provost more of a leadership role and less a managerial one. Compared to a dean or director, whose domain requires management, whatever else is also needed, provostial administration might appropriately be called abstract. To allocate funds to a dean or librarian is different from *spending* that money for faculty members or for books; to initiate policies and standards and to ensure their maintenance is not the same as *making the decisions* that implement or are in accord with those principles. We must clearly understand this administrative "level," if a provost is to steer between two perils, between an academic Scylla and Charybdis. Scylla, the monster with six long necks ending in six heads, each with three rows of pointed teeth, aptly symbolizes the more prevalent danger facing a provost: confusion introduced into the heart of decision making through a multiplication of processes. The second peril is Charybdis, the giant who swallows the waters of the sea; the academic administration that is so abstract as to empty its administrations of content. Think of a helmsman engaged in the motions of steering, where only a trickle of water flows over the ship's rudder.

The second of these perils will not require much elaboration. It consists of an almost exclusive stress on formal processes in which pieces of paper of variously prescribed sorts flow up to the provost and down to the deans without much thought lavished on their content. Form—paper in motion—substitutes for content—scrutiny and assessment of the decisions conveyed by scrupulously filled out forms. Even the bulk of the decisions that appropriate funds can be transformed into a mere formality, if later allocations are simply regarded as functions of allocations made at an earlier time. Up or down 5 percent, across the board, depending on whether we're headed into better times or worse. There's neither management nor leadership; drift takes the place of both.

We shall shortly describe some organizational features of a provost's office that help prevent this brand of underadministration. This danger, however, is incurred much less frequently than the excesses of the multi-headed beast, although the post-Homeric doctrine of sin likely accounts for the disparity. Laziness readily leads to the kind of underadministration described, but lazy academics are much less prone to become senior academic administrators than hard workers. A second sin that accounts for the abstention from effective control is vanity, for a concentration on the status and trappings of high office may lead to the ignoring of its authority. But while vanity no doubt accounts for some administrative behavior, the original and hence pervasive sin that besets humankind is pride. And most theologians agree that pride is paradigmatically expressed in the willful exercise of power, here a kind of *overmanagement.*

Although encounters with Scylla are not at all rare, some account is needed of what happens when the vision of provostial administration as "abstract" is obscured. Simply put, blindness to the difference between *supervising* decision making and actually *deciding* inevitably leads to the duplication at the higher level of the process already undertaken at the lower one. (Such a repetition is not to be confused with joint decision making, where two or more persons or agencies work toward an *agreement* as to what is to be done. Nor is such reiteration the same as the relationship of advising, which recommends, and deciding, which takes action, either following or not following the advice given.) When the situation is stated so bluntly, it may seem unbelievable that one should actually find full-fledged redundancies. Yet it is not unusual to have an agency at one level—frequently consisting of several persons—undertake an elaborate process of decision making, only to have a higher office engage in parallel substantive deliberations with its own cadre of participants, either accepting or denying the earlier decision.

Such duplication of the decision-making process makes lavish use of time and personnel. Observers, if not always participants, see the waste and wonder why they couldn't get the process right in the first place. The delays this iteration causes in provostial responses to proposals by deans and directors are all too obvious to those who are ready to act. Especially where time is of the essence, as in faculty recruiting, such enforced waiting induces counterproductive frustration or cynicism or both. A further consequence of this redundancy is still more devastating, even though it remains largely hidden from observers and participants alike. As the next maxim asserts, there is less to that duplication than meets the eye: *Maxim 19. Decisions obliged to be reached independently by more than one person or agency tend not to be attained responsibly by any of them.*

This maxim needs some explanation, for one can certainly imagine situations in which good decisions are invariably rewarded and bad ones punished, so that a repetition of decision making on a higher, supervisory level would induce conscientiousness on the lower. But in the real world, administrative processes are seldom so rigorously consistent and reliable. Duplication more often *obscures* accountability and prompts reciprocal buckpassing. Efforts on the lower level are likely to be slackened, since "they" will make their own decision anyway. But because those higher "theys" tacitly assume that the requisite deliberations had already taken place on the level below, their own efforts are sure to cut corners as well. The following truth would seem too obvious to deserve acclaiming as a maxim, except for the widespread need to use it as a reminder in academic administration: *Maxim 20. Doing something twice in a slipshod manner is not the equal of doing it meticulously once.*

In sum, instead of improving the decisions that are generated by a dual process, reiteration is likely to make them worse. And because redundant decision-making processes are employed for those decisions perceived to be the most significant, unclarity about the character of administration at the provostial level is not only wasteful and a source of frustration, but reduces the effectiveness of how some of the institution's most important decisions are arrived at. Unless an institution avoids both the Scylla of provostial overmanaging or metamanaging and the Charybdis of provostial underadminstering, the institution lacks an effective chief academic officer.

THE ABSTRACT CHARACTER OF PROVOSTIAL ADMINISTRATION

Clarity about the abstract character of provostial administration means understanding the difference between making a decision and reviewing it. The essence of the latter activity is to serve as guarantor of the decision making process. A vital precondition for reviewing a decision is the presence at the start of a clear conception of what are appropriate steps to be followed in arriving at a determination and which considerations are to be given the most serious weight. The prerequisite for making appropriate reviews of decisions is to know what a good decision is and what is a good way to get there. One might think of this as the cash value of a provost's concern with goals and policies and standards, on one side, and with procedures, on the other.

Given such a framework, to be able to review a specific decision calls for knowing how the particular decision was arrived at, so as to be informed how conscientiously evidence was gathered and weighed and how well the prescribed procedures were followed, in letter and spirit. But a review should also reveal how close the decision comes to meeting institutional standards and to achieving its goals.

Because reviewing is not deciding, a decision is overruled only if flagrant inadequacies are discovered—blatant deviations from goals or standards, procedural flaws that verge on illegality. But provostial self-restraint regarding particular reviews does not mean that their paper distillates are simply filed away for use by some possible future inspector general. Instead, the results of such reviews are in two ways central to the provost's task of overseeing the deans and directors that report to him or her, as raw material for exercising the influence-through-supervision, as suggested by *Maxim 4*. First, what is learned about how decisions are made in a unit (and of what kind) affords a perspective not readily available to the unit's day-to-day manager and helps in providing guidance for the school's or other division's standards and directions. And second, the same findings play a significant role in the evaluation of the unit's head; they become part of the basis for praise and blame, together with their tangible manifestations, ranging from substantial salary raises to none or to dismissal, the ultimate reprimand.

[4] To what position a given officer reports significantly affects the way in which his or her responsibilities are discharged.

To sum up, the provost does not review the decisions made in the schools and units that report to that office in order to challenge each one of them and to try to get it improved, but in order to create a situation where those who have the responsibility for making decisions make good decisions *in an ongoing way*. This kind of oversight is a significant managerial tool for the exercise of the provost's academic leadership functions. For the provost's support of the academic enterprise aims at ensuring that primary academic administrators and heads of supporting units, such as libraries, do their jobs effectively, that they move their domains toward agreed-upon goals and do so in conformity with institutional policies and standards.

THE PROVOST'S STAFF

Given the centrality of the kind of oversight just described, a provost must accord high priority to the possession of information. In organizing an office capable of providing it, the need for three kinds of specialist dominates: one concerning financial matters, a second knowledgeable about space and its use, and a third versed in faculty affairs. While furnishing information is indeed the principal responsibility of each of these staff officers, it would be somewhat disingenuous to represent them as a species of research assistant. Although none of these staff members is given much scope for decision making, all must possess considerable expertise and, in their capacity as special advisors to the provost, broad experience and good judgment.

Maxim 8 reminds us of the ubiquity of budgetary decisions, so we begin with money. Although enjoined not to spend the funds they allocate, provosts must know with precision and timeliness how those allocations are spent by the units that report to them. The receipt of a variety of formulations of financial data provide insight into fiscal decisions made in given units and also bear on the broader picture needed at the vice presidential level. A provostial staff budget officer is a necessity.

[8] *Few significant campus decisions are without budgetary implications.*

We turn next to the use of space, along with its renovation and modification. Although dedicated to the life of the mind, nothing arouses greater emotion among faculty members than issues of space. While the depth of these feelings may have roots in some prerational territorial instinct, there is often (though not always) justification for passion, since how well an academic unit thrives may depend on the magnitude and quality of its space. At the same time, greed creates a shortage of space even in the rarest of cases where objective reality does not, sharpening the need for optimizing the use of available space and adjudicating sagaciously among competing demands—where sagacity amounts to disposing of space in accord with institutional academic priorities. Clearly, a provost needs the assistance of someone who possess familiarity and experience both with the operation of academic programs and the intricacies of space and its use.

Whether the provost is or is not the institution's chief operating officer will not make as much difference to these positions of provostial budget and space advisors as one might think. What does differ is the provost's power to determine how the entire institution employs its resources. The heating plant, the development office, and almost every other support unit will at some time claim to need more space, while, most certainly, every one of them will put in for significant budget increases. Whether the provost only pleads the case of the academic side—while a business vice president supports the claims of the nonacademic units—or whether the provost actually determines how much goes where throughout the institution, can make a substantial difference in the way that resources are allocated. As chief operating officer, the provost can in principle call on the services of the entire business staff; this fact does not obviate the need for the kind of specialized provostial advisors just considered. Whatever the organizational scheme, nothing changes regarding the need for budget and space persons who are thoroughly versed in the operations and perspectives of *academic* units and capable of providing information and advice to the provost and of serving as interpreters between the business offices for budget and space and the institution's academic units.

The main function of the third staff member indispensable in a provost's office is to monitor the personnel decisions of the academic units. Answers to the questions as to who is hired and how, what salaries are set and in accordance with what principles of dispersion, who is reappointed, promoted, or dismissed and on the basis of what criteria and procedures reveal how satisfactorily deans and directors implement institutional policies. Attention must of course be paid to the meticulousness with which mandated procedures are followed—not only for the sake of bureaucratic discipline, but because more than one institutional regulation fulfills legal requirements as well. But while the provost's assistant must therefore possess technical competence and a temperament capable of coping with detail, much more is needed than fastidiousness. Bureaucratic processes, however important they may be, must not be permitted to take on greater significance than the goals they are meant to bring about. The provostial advisor on personnel decisions must possess the judgment capable of assessing the quality of those decisions. What is needed, then, is prior experience with—indeed, substantial participation in—decisions about hiring and promoting faculty members as requisite for the kind of "feel" (or wisdom) needed in the assessment of deanly decisions. Senior faculty members who might want to conclude their careers by providing administrative help to their institutions constitute a useful source for fulfilling such provostial staff functions.

In large universities and even in smaller but variegated settings, there may be a need for additional staff persons—from specialists in appeals procedures and problems of retirement and emeriti to keepers of faculty records. In any of these areas, a single staff officer is sufficient in one institution, while more substantial offices are needed in others. The limits of the size and elaborateness of the office of the provost are set by Maxim 2, which requires that any component be justifiable by a (needed!) goal it accomplishes. Unreasonably large offices can be avoided if in the promulgation of institutional procedures the provost has paid heed to the following maxim: *Maxim 21. Refrain from making rules that make normal business more difficult merely in order to prevent*

[2] Some means cannot be justified by any end; nevertheless, the only way in which a means can be justified at all is by showing that it contributes to bringing about a desired end.

offenses that might be committed on rare occasions. To make normal business more cumbersome by engaging in defensive administration gobbles up personnel whose job becomes that of checking on the work of the checkers. People are thus actually deployed to reduce the clarity and efficiency of decision making—a crew, moreover (or the payroll that supports it) that could be put to constructive use.

WHERE THE REALM IS TOO LARGE

In the discussion of all these members of the provost's office, we have placed stress on their nature as staff positions, even if some of them bear such resounding titles as associate provost for fiscal affairs or faculty affairs or the like. Tacit in this emphasis is the assumption that the provost supervises in person the deans of the schools and heads of other units that report to him or her. Where the abstractness of administration at the provost's level is taken seriously, such relatively lean offices should in many cases be possible, perhaps with a personal provost's assistant fielding questions and requests about uneliminable detail. If the provost does not play super-dean, metamanaging the management of deans and directors, supervision can and should above all consist of periodic meetings of provost and each unit head—sometimes with and sometimes without other staff members present. During these encounters, recent and prospective developments are the chief agenda items, discussed within the three-fold context of the *goals* of the school or other facility, of the *relationships and interactions*, actual and desirable, between that unit and others, and, of the needs and availability of *resources*. Given recurrent meetings of this kind, it should be possible to limit other interactions between supervisor and supervised and allow the provost to oversee a fair number of schools and other units. Indeed, it should be possible for the provost to attend to the many nonroutine duties that, without fail, usurp time and energy set aside for something else. With luck, it should even be feasible for the provost to meet from time to time with the faculties of schools and departments so as to get a first-hand understanding of the ambitions and concerns that prevail in his or her domain.

This account of the organization of the office of the provost has been faithful to the conception of provost as leader, as someone who influences the directions to be taken by the institution's schools, centers, and para-academic units, backed up by the power of the purse and authority over the heads of these units. While some actual provost's offices resemble the picture here put forward, other citizens of the real world will wistfully pine after such a scene, seeing it as irredeemably utopian. One category of provost is simply too heavily burdened with management obligations to maintain offices that conform to the model put forward; another has too large a number of officers to supervise to cope in this way; while a third is saddled with both of these afflictions.

There is no single path out from under such handicaps and no doubt each of the ways to be briefly sketched requires compromising with some pertinent principle. But one route is to be avoided, since it gives up altogether on the basic conception of the provostial role here advocated. In the face of pressures that overwhelm, a provost might create a number of associate provostships, to each of whom a group of deans and directors reports. This scheme, patterned after the organization of a large dean's office, is open to two possibilities, both of them undesirable. The first makes the main job of these associate provosts that of co-managing the enterprises of the persons overseen, while the provost retains the supervisory role earlier put forward. This pattern, appropriate at the dean's level, fully undermines the thesis of the abstractness of administration at the provostial level. The second alternative has associate provosts allowing the persons they oversee manage their own units and refraining from bureaucratic metamanaging, which leaves the provost's subordinates to supervise the group of deans and directors assigned to them in the manner previously proposed for the provost. If so, associate provosts become *de facto* mini-provosts, with the titular provost, floating above them like a cloud, faced with the necessity of stitching together an all-institution perspective from the pieces that organization has split apart. In sum, this approach makes it exceedingly difficult for a provost to exercise the appropriate leadership role.

If delegating authority to a group of associate provosts is not the solution to the problems that led to the consideration of such posts; these difficulties have not suddenly gone away. There indeed are provosts too heavily occupied with management activities. One message to them is brutally simple: reduce your managing activities by eliminating redundant processes and by delegating to the deans and directors you have appointed. Let them do their jobs and draw the consequences if they don't perform adequately. But don't allow your leadership role to be bogged down: if you don't perform it, no one else will.

Yet this message does not help where laws, system-wide regulations, or board of trustee directives *require* the provost to check on the checkers. To them goes a second message: assign different necessary managerial tasks to yet more assistants who will perform them as specialists in various administrative processes. Let these qualified assistants—if need be, more in number than the cadre earlier proposed—do most of the managing for you. Since the solution here is to assign managerial tasks to specialists hired to perform them—rather than eliminating them altogether—the compromise is with the principle of the abstractness of provostial administration. It may further be necessary to appoint a deputy or chief of staff to supervise so large a group of assistants, but, in spite of obstacles, the provost might in this way still be capable of performing the primary leadership functions that no one else can take on.

That leaves the problem of provosts who cannot perform their jobs, simply because the number of units reporting to them is larger than any one person can handle. Supervising is work, says Maxim 5, a fact that sets a limit to the number of persons to whom meaningful direction can be given. When that number is exceeded (and it will vary, if only because the nature of the assignments of those who are supervised also matters), there will be a certain amount of pseudo-supervision, with potentially unhappy results, as discussed in Chapter 1. Where there is a prospect of being overwhelmed by numbers, the provost's leadership function must nevertheless not be sacrificed by parcelling out the position to a group of associates. Instead, reporting lines must be rethought to make the provost's job doable.

[5] Supervising is work, calling for the dedication of time, energy, and know-how.

In principle, all academic units should report to the provost, where "academic" is understood in the broadest sense. This is the principle that may well have to be sacrificed to solve the problem of numbers. To accommodate the multiversity, it may be necessary to move from a broader to a narrower conception of the academic realm, so that provostial leadership can be given to the remaining center of the academic enterprise, instead of being sacrificed to a vain attempt to deal with its entirety. The need to shrink the provost's realm may tell us something about advisability of developing those multiversities; but instead of wishing that reality were different from what it is, one job of the next chapter will be to consider alternative reporting lines for those offices that would, in an ideal world, report to the provost. Remember, in conclusion here, where the provost does not provide academic leadership to the institution as a whole, no one else will do so.

CHAPTER 5
Some Other Units

THE HEALTH SCIENCES

In Plato's *Statesman*, the Eleatic Stranger chides young Socrates for dividing humankind into two classes, Greeks and barbarians, with the latter term meaning no more than "foreigners" or "all others." Those barbarians, after all, share no characteristics by virtue of which they belong to the same class. Things are in slightly better shape in this chapter, because we will primarily be considering administrators for whom there is a *prima facie* case for reporting to the provost. But we won't consider *all* such officers nor *only* that kind, so that I would be forced to respond to a contemporary Stranger that the collectivity to be discussed shares the peculiar trait of being thought by me to be usefully considered. For this primer—not intended to be a complete handbook—this means a selection of topics that are important for the governance of academic institutions or for the significance of the lessons for good government that can be learned from their consideration. We turn to look at *some other* administrators, in the hope that they measure up to one or both of these criteria.

The previous chapter took for granted that all deans of colleges and schools must report to the provost, since overseeing their operations is at the center of the chief academic officer's role. Nevertheless, a group of possible exceptions must be considered: deans of medical and other health science schools. Most everyone knows the joke about the college president standing before St. Peter, who reverses the decision to send him to the nether regions when he hears that the president oversaw an institution that had *two* medical schools. Extenuating circumstances. The size and complexity, along every dimension, of many medical organizations, and the sharp and deep differences from most other university units regarding fiscal underpinnings and mores, make one wonder whether they are at all *in* or *a part of* a university in the way other schools and colleges are. Such realities must be faced, although it is worthwhile to consider first what would be ideal.

A provost, to begin with, would be as responsible for the standards of health-related academic programs and of the faculty carrying them out as for any other in the university. The provost, further, would have an influence over the directions in which such programs develop, considering the strengths of the units in question, the directions in which their fields were tending, together with the relationship of these to the goals of the university considered as a whole. In particular, the provost would serve as an agent who fosters collaboration and complementarity—rather than competition and duplication—especially between life science research in the medical context and in that of biological sciences within the arts and sciences unit. Finally, the provost would be able to treat the health science budget as "just another part" of the university budget, no more or less subject to provostial modification than the budget of any other major university unit.

At a university of modest size, sporting a compact medical school unembellished with hospitals, it may be possible to have the dean of that school report to the provost and to have that chief academic officer provide the kind of ongoing guidance described in the previous paragraph. But this is surely the exception. Where the medical school is large, where there are several other health profession schools, where there is a hospital complex, any reporting to the provost by the heads of these units is likely to be more apparent than real, with a provost unlikely to be able to cope with what it takes to supervise, as suggested

[5] Supervising is work, calling for the dedication of time, energy, and know-how.

by *Maxim 5*. For practical purposes, the result, as already observed more than once, is an *un*supervised part of the institution, in this case a mighty and sprawling one.

The first element in a resolution of so undesirable a condition is the presence of an officer who oversees the many tentacles of a large health science complex. Its academic and clinical programs must be coordinated with each other and some order must be infused into the management of relations with diverse parts and levels of government and the community, as well as with donors. To such a person—presumably a vice president for health sciences—the heads of the different health-related units report, thus acknowledging organizationally the singular place of the medical establishment within the university.

The second component in the "placement" of the health sciences into the university is to determine to whom their vice president is, in turn, to report. The disproportionate size of the collective budgets of these units and both the importance and complexity of their relationships to various extramural worlds, make it plausible for the health science vice president to report directly to the head of the institution. If, instead, the provost is the formal supervisor of the medical vice president, an unhelpful ambiguity is in all likelihood introduced into the reporting relationship, given that president and health science chief have so much business they must conduct jointly. Again, a concession to reality is preferable to obscuring it.

While, in effect, this reporting relationship acknowledges the anomalous role played by a large medical establishment within the university, there is a special need to provide centripetal forces. Thus, even for health science schools, the provost must be chief *academic* officer, whose standards and policies pertain to the appointment and promotion of health science faculties and academic programs. No doubt, at times, a president will require considerable fortitude to resist reversing a provostial decision that overruled one made by the health science vice president. No doubt, too, a president will at times be required to adjudicate between these two senior officers, since there will be occasions when they will fail to agree on the deployment of life science faculty and facilities within the university, not to mention inevitable budgetary disputes. In short, special awareness is needed to prevent a medical establishment from moving out of its university housing altogether, if only not in name.

STUDENT AFFAIRS

Unlike universities on the European continent, American colleges and universities are concerned with the lives of their students outside the classroom—at least during their stay on campus. We say that *in loco parentis* is a practice of the past, but that is so only if we look at parents in their role as administrators of behavioral restrictions, where, with respect to late adolescents, there may, in any case, not be much left to be *in loco* of, since parents themselves have ceased to be *parentalis*. But if we think of parents as providers of care and numerous services needed or desirable for living, our academic institutions still do much parenting, most or all of it carried out under the aegis of someone with a title such as vice president for student affairs.

Undergraduates living in student housing on campus receive the greatest attention from the office of student affairs. Therefore, in order to get a good grasp of its functions, here is a brief account of what such an office does at their maximal level, with the understanding that nonresident students, part time students, and graduate students receive fewer services from that office and that some of the functions indicated may at some institutions be assigned to other offices. The first function is the provision of housing and food, usually managed as break-even businesses. A second major function is to provide and supervise a range of extracurricular and recreational activities, both associated with and independent of student residences. The range of these may be large, from supervising athletic and fitness-related activities to managing theatrical and musical activities and facilities. Many campuses have fraternities and sororities to be supervised, and all have a student government to be overseen. Academic institutions also minister to their students' bodies and souls by providing medical services and psychological counseling, and they give students a helping hand toward their futures by means of a job placement service.

This batch of functions seems to be *sui generis*; different from anything else on campus; the people carrying out these functions require their own kind of training and skills. It is thus easy to conclude that it should not much matter who oversees the chief of student life or even that it might best be the business vice president, since so much business is, literally, involved in managing residences and food services. In any case, it is easy to conclude that student affairs are properly regarded as *parallel* to academic affairs, to be so treated in a similar way organizationally. Two cultures, after all, can and should live side by side, the academic one and that of recreation, broadly as well as etymologically understood.

And yet, things are more complicated than this picture suggests. On many a campus, the activities for which student affairs are responsible contribute as much or more to the institution's ethos than does the academic enterprise. On all campuses, how these affairs are conducted teaches what is valuable and important and what is or is not desirable, and encourages behavior of this sort rather than that; student life purveys what has aptly been named a hidden curriculum. It is not a given, then, that the two cultures sit side by side, indifferent to each other. Instead, various practices of student affairs may compete and conflict with the goals of the academic enterprise or may complement and support its pedagogic aims.

However desirable this last tendency may be, an ideological corollary of *Maxim 1* suggests that natural forces won't foster it, that art is needed to try to bring it about. Reporting lines, therefore, do matter: the person who oversees the officer who directs student affairs on a given campus must *care* that these affairs are conducted in ways that are supportive of the academic enterprise and must have an *understanding* as to what that might mean. The chief academic officer is the most obviously equipped to combat centrifugality in this domain. The guidance an academic administrator gives to a vice president for student affairs, the sort of practices he or she encourages and supports or discourages and thwarts should at least help to reduce the conflict between those two campus cultures, if not achieve more positive results.

[1] *In academic institutions, the forces of nature are centrifugal; organizational art must be used to create propensities toward coherence.*

The least unsatisfactory alternative to this arrangement is to have the head of student affairs report directly to the president. This is particularly appropriate at a smaller institution, where primary and chief academic administrator are the same person, namely, the dean of the faculty. It is preferable even at a large institution—assuming the number of deans and heads of units reporting to the provost is large—to relegating student affairs to the business side of the institution, with its head reporting to the business vice president. Indeed, the most acceptable departure from the ideal may be the retention of the reporting line from head of student affairs to chief academic officer, while reluctantly accepting the price of inadequate supervision. In this way, the academic enterprise retains at least this influence over student life on campus: that the chief of the former exercises the determinative influence as to who will serve as the head of the latter.

GRADUATE EDUCATION AND RESEARCH

In contrast to more homogeneous liberal arts colleges, the two layers of academic dean and provost are inevitable in institutions engaged in two ventures that are normally found together and certainly should be: graduate education and research. In determining the distribution of administrative functions in these two provinces, the same principles that distinguish the roles of dean and provost apply. The matter of resources, as always, is central and flexibility is an ingredient in the effectiveness with which they might be used. This consideration suggests that funds for graduate fellowships, stipends for teaching and research assistants, together with the funds to remit the tuition of graduate students be retained at the level of the central administration for distribution to different units engaged in graduate education in ways that further an institution's strategy in this educational terrain. Similarly, the pooling, at the vice presidential level, of start-up funds and other resources for the support of research (including the provision of time released from teaching duties) most readily permits the support of research in accord with perceptions of its quality and in conformity with institutional policies and goals.

If these considerations weigh on the side of not simply decentralizing the administration of graduate education and research, so does the need for spokespersons for these functions in the corridors of power. What policies further or hinder the peculiar activity of graduate education and the great diversity of the conduct of research is best understood by those in daily contact with those engaged in these activities. Broad policy and fiscal decisions can importantly affect these areas in ways that are not readily detected by administrators who are not truly conversant with them, making second-hand advocacy less than second best.

Still, neither the corridor in which the graduate nor the research administrator resides should lead directly into the presidential suite. While presidents are seldom tempted to have graduate deans report directly to them, there are certainly many examples of vice presidents for research who are directly supervised by the institution's head. Such a structure harbors two potential dangers, assuming the goal of assuring the primacy of the academic enterprise. First, research activity is clearly a central component of that undertaking. Therefore, if that province is overseen by a senior officer who is essentially parallel to the chief academic officer, the administration of the academic realm is divided, with the power and authority of the provost diminished.

The second risk amounts to a possible consequence of the first. Research vice presidents who are not under the supervision of the chief academic officer are more likely to foster research projects and ventures that are *not* of particular relevance to the research of the professoriate and its students. When one has a garden of one's own, there is a temptation to cultivate it as best one can, with stress on the profusion of its flowers, rather than on discrimination among species. There may well be significant opportunities to engage in applied research and technology transfer and to create flourishing research centers devoted to such pursuits. Although it is not an appropriate topic for this book to discuss when it might or might not be desirable for a university to pursue such directions, it is germane to note that a confusion of activities that are *not* pertinent to the academic enterprise with those that *are* quickly translates into an expenditure of funds that diminish what is available for those central purposes of the university. The creation of a research vice presidency independent of the chief academic officer invites precisely that kind of confusion, making likely an almost inadvertent diminution of the fostering of academically relevant research.

The alternative to such confusion is the clarity that is achieved when the two functions that go under the name of "research" are embodied in two different advocates, wherever the pursuit of both of them is wanted. One, an officer who reports to the president, is concerned with applied research, perhaps oriented toward for-profit establishments or the community, while the second, an officer who reports to the provost, is given the charge of nurturing and overseeing academic research. Tensions are inevitable, but at least this organizational scheme encourages open discussion.

Both the overseeing of research and of graduate study are thus functions that should be supervised by the provost. Indeed, they are often best combined as the duties of a single person, if only because graduate students are an important resource for the conduct of research, while engaging in significant research is a vital part of graduate education. If uniting those two functions in one office seems to prescribe a cruel overburdening of an academic administrator, that pang of conscience should be directed, instead, against the sin of micromanaging— the real cause of such a hardship. The person or persons charged with overseeing research and graduate study must act at a similar level of abstraction as the provost. The primary functions are those of allocation, support, advocacy, and the formation of policies. But the *formation* of policies is not the *executing* of them; the *supervision* of decisions is not the *making* of them.

The second set of these pairs of tasks belongs to the colleges and schools and to departments, where the activities of graduate education and research are located. What was noted when we contrasted the roles of deans and provosts applies here. Decisions made at too "high" a level are undertaken without adequate information and sensitivity to the specific situations to which they apply; at best, they are "merely" redundant. At the same time, because they interfere with an appropriate measure of autonomy on the "lower" level, such constraints sow confusion into the evaluation of those being supervised and therefore undermine efforts to make line administrators truly responsible for their actions.

In Chapter 4 we mentioned research centers as academic units that are often in particular need of administrative support and protection because they tend to depend on the cooperation of schools that are led by deans, who, for any number of reasons, are more powerful administrators than center directors. Many a provost, however, has too full a plate to give such multidisciplinary units the attention they should have. Given these centers' function as *research* units, with financing from sources similar to those that support research by individual faculty members and by groups that are wholly housed within schools, the vice president for research makes a perfectly plausible supervisor.

PARA-ACADEMIC UNITS

The broad rubric of "para-academic" distinguishes two kinds of units found in colleges and universities. The first exists to *support* the primary functions of teaching and research and would not be found on campus were that not so. The second kind might be thought of as *parallel* to the principal academic enterprise and much more loosely related to it. We will take these up in turn.

Two organizations that directly support the academic enterprise were mentioned in the previous chapter: the library and computing services. No institution is without the first and few are now without the latter. Accordingly, we can let them serve as samples of other facilities—such as certain laboratories and major instrumentation facilities—that transcend school boundaries and similarly assist both faculty members and students in research and teaching. As so often before, the importance of *Maxim 4* creates a *prima facie* bias in favor of having the directors of these facilities report to the provost. The underlying principle is simple: let the same office that gives direction to the academic enterprise also supervise operations that are indispensable aids in their conduct, with a view to keeping this goal paramount.

[4] *To what position a given officer reports significantly affects the way in which his or her responsibilities are discharged.*

This advice may make perfectly good sense, but how important is following it, especially when faced with an overburdened provost? Why does it matter at all, since there doesn't seem anything else for these para-academic units to do, except to support the work of faculty and students? For two reasons, these questions are not rhetorical. The first is mundane and uncomplicated: there is much need for coordination. As teaching and research programs change, as disciplines are added and dropped, the nature of the needed support changes as well. Communication and responsiveness are much facilitated by having the service organization housed under the same roof as the one served. More pointedly, we are here confronting a paradigmatic application of *Maxim* 8, which reminds us that academic decisions have budgetary implications. The cultivation of a new field in the classroom calls either for a shifting or an addition of resources in the library; a substantial increase of the number of students calls for variously increased capacities in the units that support their work. In all such cases, resources are more efficiently allocated where there is no need to negotiate across administrative boundaries.

[8] *Few significant campus decisions are without budgetary implications.*

The second reason as to why it matters who oversees these supporting para-academic units is rooted in the fact that they *are* capable of going astray. Just as one made fun of old fashioned librarians who preferred seeing books neatly standing on their shelves to having them in the hands of readers, so entire libraries and other facilities can develop goals of their own that are in direct conflict with the best interests of their users. Although for their users, libraries are *means*, they are in an important way *ends* to those who run them. What makes a better library to which they aspire and work towards, what constitutes success in rivalries among "competing" libraries need not include better service to their users and more successful support of teaching and research. (Statistics about academic libraries seldom include numbers of users and never, to my knowledge, an assessment of how satisfied they are.) Accordingly, to contain such impulses to become an end-in-itself and to keep supporting units harnessed to the institutional goals they are meant to serve, the supervisor must know well what those goals are and be responsible for furthering them.

Before drawing some organizational consequences from such observations, I want to take a brief glance at a different kind of supporting unit, if only to point to some underlying similarities. The office of the registrar is not populated by professionals possessing advanced degrees, as many a library or computer service is, and what that office does resembles a business function far more than it resembles what professors and students do. And yet, the way courses are numbered and how their availability is made known to students, the time slots and rooms to which they are assigned, and the degree of ease or difficulty with which students' educational plans can be implemented when it is time to register for courses all have a significant effect on the academic lives of students.

To facilitate smooth coordination is a reason to have this supporting organization report to the same person who oversees the enterprise being served. But here, too, the second reason applies as well. In another context, we noted the operation of *Maxim 15*. Something analogous can easily happen to the office of a registrar. Instead of devising methods that have as a primary goal the enabling of students to make the most effective and timely educational choices, that goal is readily subordinated to one that serves the registrar's office itself. The resulting registration system would then aim, above all, at making the job of registering and keeping track easier for those who do it, sacrificing effectiveness of service to student-clients.

[15] An office that lacks goals of its own will tend to give priority to getting the process right over getting the job done.

Other things being equal, such a shift in aim is more likely to be fostered by a business supervisor, for whom efficiency must be a guiding principle than by a supervisor who is charged with nurturing the academic enterprise. The office of the registrar is organizationally similar to the library and computing services; if it was not *obvious* that the registrar should report to the provost, this organizational relationship makes sense upon reflection.

All this may well leave us with the problem of the overworked provost. Here, however, delegation to an associate is far more plausible than for the supervision of primary academic units, such as schools and colleges—assuming effective communication among the members of the office of the provost. The influence of the academic enterprise on the library, computing services, registrar, and other supporting para-academic units must also come from what might be called "user committees." The committees articulate the needs of the library's or registrar's clients to whoever supervises them, provost or associate provost, to serve as advocates, and to help formulate policies sensitive to the needs of users.

A second type of para-academic unit is more loosely and variously related to central academic processes. An art gallery, an anthropological museum, a university press can function, to varying degrees, as instruments of public relations, with the primary role of reaching out to a larger lay world. On the other hand, such units might, in different ways and to varying degrees, play a role in ongoing teaching and research.

And the appropriate reporting line shifts accordingly. If priority is given to the scholarly quality of such an establishment and to its relationship to the institution's teaching and research, its director must report to an academic officer. Again, provost, associate provost, or research vice president are the plausible candidates, essentially for reasons already stated. But if such a unit is just another component in a multiversity, with few ties to academic programs, an overburdened provost's office might be relieved by a business vice president. At a smaller school, where the dean doubles as chief academic officer, it might even be appropriate to have the president oversee a press or a museum.

Still, para-academic units must retain an academic character if they are to represent a college or university in a fitting manner. Accordingly, regardless of reporting lines, the provost—or an academic officer designated by the provost—must be centrally involved in the selection of the head of these kinds of units. Finally, each such enterprise must be guided by a committee dominated by faculty members knowledgeable about its domain.

This last paragraph suggests a concluding word—before *some* other units become *all* others. The danger of discussing every adminstrator to be found on campus exists, because it is surely the case that every unit in a college or university must represent its campus in a way that befits an *academic* institution. Moreover, the earlier point that the student life establishment purveys a hidden curriculum can readily be generalized. The interactions students have with *any* part of their college or university tells them something about what this institution thinks of them and their role. The policies and practices of any campus component with which students come in contact induce patterns of behavior in those students and, as a part of an academic institution, thus become willy nilly involved in teaching. There are the makings of an argument here that all units that are not academic units be counted among the para-academic ones.

Still, we had better keep our megalomania in check. What might be implied for the organization of an academic institution, were one to give in to such impulses, could not be implemented in any but the smallest and simplest one. For to have a chief academic officer attempt to do everything is surely to doom that officer to doing nothing right. Nevertheless, all the components of an academic institution *do* represent it to the world; almost every unit within it *is* tacitly engaged in teaching. It becomes the responsibility of an institution's entire leadership, from president on down, to select personnel and to encourage policies that reflect the special nature of colleges and universities.

CHAPTER 6
Departmental Organization

THE GOOD DEPARTMENT AND SOME OBSTACLES
TO ACHIEVING IT

After six chapters of talk, we finally turn to discuss those units that do the bulk of the work for which academic institutions exist. We are speaking of units, supervised by a dean, that consist of faculty members who are engaged in teaching, research, and serving as mentors to students, undergraduate and advanced. Some of these divisions are programs, usually organized to accomplish a specific educational purpose. Most of them are departments that house faculty members by discipline. These latter are the main subject of this chapter and it is with them that we begin.

Other things being equal, wise observers of the academy have noted the following: *Maxim 22. Over time, good departments get better, while bad departments get worse.* Academic administration (with its resources) ranks highest among the determinants that make things *un*equal. Its job, clearly, is to foster or at least get out of the way of the good department and to work against deterioration of the bad department, depending on the starting point. Neither of these tasks is easy. But before we can explore the bearing of organizational features on the achievement of favorable results, something must be said about what it is for a department to be good and what the chief obstacles are that stand in the way of the development or perpetuation of a good department.

It is tempting to cut this discussion short by saying that a department is precisely as good as the individual members of which it is composed. After all, what more could one ask for than an assemblage of Nobelists and members of prestigious national and international societies that signal attainment of the apex of a profession? But there are several traps in this conventional measure of departmental excellence and whatever college or university ignores these snares is less effective in carrying out its mission than it might be.

First, since such glorious companies are nearly as rare as hens' teeth, it matters that one cannot easily extrapolate downward from these apexes of the different professions. Various ranking schemes have been devised to measure scholarly standing, but they are best at the rank ordering of productivity, which largely leaves out depth, importance, originality, and imaginativeness. These rankings are thus not firmly related to the actual mission of the employing institution. Moreover, this tack tacitly assumes—wrongly, for most institutions—that research is its only mission. Finally, this approach is simplistic, if not naive, because it fails to recognize that with respect to any mission, a department as a whole can be more or less than the sum of the individuals that are its parts.

None of this is intended to deny that good departments are made up of people who are good at the teaching, research, advising, mentoring, and clinical practice required by the institution's mission. But it does suggest a focus beyond individuals, since it matters that the *group* contains an appropriate mix of these functions. It requires a *corporate* conception of the way a discipline is represented within a department— with the degree of "coverage" of its subspecialties appropriate to the scale of the department's college or university. Finally, the quality of a department depends in part upon the role it plays in the institution of which it is a part. To consider only research productivity fails to do justice to the complex role of individual faculty members. Analogously, to look only at research, while refraining from assessing a department for the contribution it makes, among other things, to interdisciplinary teaching and research programs and to the formulation and implementation of the institution's educational policies, is to confuse an academic deapartment with a free-standing research institute.

If this constitutes an overview of what one might want a department to *be*, one must not overlook its capacity to *become*. A good department *is* one that becomes better; its decision making fosters not only the goals just mentioned, but assures that the department remains at the forefront of its discipline, importing new skills and knowledge with each new appointment. Whatever subspecialties may constitute the appropriate province of a given department, it must, as a unit, both preserve the basic core of its discipline and have the capacity to be creative at its frontiers.

As everybody knows, the unavailability of an adequate budget or, in some fields, of facilities—relative to the ambition and status of the institution—is a serious, though not always fatal obstacle to the achievement of departmental ambitions. Nothing we can say here will solve this ubiquitous problem. Instead, I want to cite three types of departmental afflictions for which administration can at least provide a partial cure, though nothing, alas, about the etiology of these diseases prevents a department from contracting all three of them.

The first is simply an instantiation of *Maxim 22.* Mediocrity tends to perpetuate itself in its personnel decisions, either because of an inability

[22] Over time, good departments get better, while bad departments get worse.

to discern what is excellent or, more likely, because it fears the competition from greater talent, more energy, and a more dedicated sense of purpose. As the following maxim indicates, only the best seeks out the best: *Maxim 23. "A" people hire (or retain) "A" people, while "B" people hire "C" people.*

A second obstacle to departmental excellence stems from certain kinds of ideological splits that politicize personnel and curricular decisions and make students victims of warring factions. The term "ideological" is not here limited to such humanities phenomena as the battle between traditionalism and multiculturalism, although that is an example. As used here, the term accepts the possibility for all fields, including the most rigorous sciences, to have differences in style or approach that give rise to hardened factions. In mathematics, the more theoretical and the more applied may not be able to live peacefully together; in some of the empirical sciences, the theoretical and the experimental may come to oppose rather than complement each other; mathematical approaches may be spurned by qualitative biologists or vice versa, and a similar division can crop up in departments of sociology. What one might call the anthropology of scholarship will always produce passionate antagonisms—and not merely of the old versus the new—that convert academic decision making into political squabbles.

A third kind of dysfunctional department is one that is simply *non*-functional as a department. This academic unit becomes a locus where individuals hang their hats, move out from to teach their classes, receive their mail and, especially, their salary checks. The individuals who make up such quasi-departments may or may not have significant scholarly careers. They perform only those departmental and other institutional duties which they cannot shirk, and then only with minimalistic sparseness.

THE NEED FOR COMMUNICATION AND THE SELECTION OF A CHAIRPERSON

More could be said about well-functioning departments and much more about the ways in which departments can deviate from excellence, but it is time to turn to the organizational matters that are the subject of this book. Our first task is to look at the governance of departments under "normal" circumstances. The aim is to obtain a condition that enables coping with departments on various levels of the ladder of virtue. On the one hand, it must permit meritorious departments to go their own way. This does not mean refraining from supervision, since the governance of even the best departments must remain open to supervision to ensure that the purposes of all component parts are ever coordinated with those of the whole. On the other hand, departmental supervision must be able to influence less perfect departments to improve as needed.

The familiar system of rotating chairpersons, as distinguished from headships with indefinite terms, brings with it two advantages for these other-things-being-equal situations. First, a faculty member is able to serve a term of three to five years without losing his or her status and *capability* as a faculty member. Since the important aspect of departmental leadership is intellectual rather than bureaucratic, it matters that potential chairpersons are not eliminated because some people quite reasonably worry about jeopardizing their careers as teachers and scholars. No doubt, good management is important for the welfare of a department, especially where that enterprise includes a significant establishment of staff, laboratories, equipment, and the like. But, as has repeatedly been observed, management can frequently be turned over to someone else—to a professional manager, budget permitting; to an assistant chairperson; or, as often in smaller circumstances, to an experienced departmental secretary. As *Maxim 3* proclaims, academic administrators do not *manage* faculty members.

[3] Academic administrators do not manage *units composed of faculty or students, however much they may at times dream of doing so.*

Two crucial functions are simply not performed, where a department's chairperson does not carry them out. Reflection by its membership about the department's pedagogic and research roles is not articulated and brought together—or even stimulated in the first place. It is thus perfectly possible that a group of people more or less successfully doing their own thing may never be welded into a unit with a set of corporate purposes. Second, without leadership from the chairperson, departmental goals and needs (as well as those of individual members) are not adequately conveyed to the institution's administration, most certainly not as embedded in an interpretation of the nature and direction of the departmental disciplines.

Because these functions are carried out automatically in such familiar organizations as business corporations, their importance in academic institutions is easily underestimated. Whatever the subunit in a corporate structure, the people who make it up "report" to their director in ways no faculty member is responsible to a chairperson or even head. The goals of each individual are derived from the goals of the unit and not, as is true to a significant extent in the academy, vice versa. (This does not mean that the tasks of the head of a corporate unit are easy to accomplish, merely that they are different.)

An analogous difference obtains when an academic department is compared to a corporate unit from the perspective of the administrative level "above" it. The purposes of a corporate division precede in every sense its actual existence. No one needs to tell corporate headquarters what the engineering division, the public relations, or legal departments are *for*, since that administration created them to accomplish tasks *they* had in mind. Although even this setting has a need to convey departmental requirements to those who have the power or budget to meet them, the explanatory function is minimal compared to that in the academy. Both in corporations and in the academy there is a need to explain a unit's activities and problems to the officer to whom its head reports, a job analogous to interpreting the ways of man to god. In this task, the corporate explicator has a much easier time of it.

Much earlier, academic institutions were characterized as essentially decentralized. *Maxim 1* operates even *within* its many different departments; without countervailing activity, those faculty members—who resemble independent contractors—can themselves be most powerful centrifugal forces. Accordingly, the exercise of the chairperson's functions, as just described, is a vital component of the art that holds the institution together. Neither the whole college or university, nor its di-

[1] In academic institutions, the forces of nature are centrifugal; organizational art must be used to create propensities toward coherence.

verse departmental parts, can survive without each other. Some glue is needed to resist those centrifugal forces and it is simply more evidence of these forces that exasperation should from time to time delude both faculty members and administrators into believing that they can survive without each other.

Given the chairperson's functions here singled out, effective communication and decision making *within* a department is an important necessary condition, suggesting that different departments be permitted to proceed in accordance with the different mores of the diverse fields. At the same time, the need for adequate communication from department to central administration suggests that mores that pertain to different fields or that result from specific histories be in two ways constrained. First, except in certain personnel decisions to be discussed below, all regular department members should have the opportunity to be heard before a conclusion is reached and, second, in all reasonably significant matters, it should be possible to discern the chairperson's position as a voice distinct from that of a departmental majority, even when holding the majority view.

If, in the peculiar theology of the academy, the ways of man need to be interpreted to god, it almost goes without saying that the conventional direction must obtain as well and the ways of god be explained to men. Besides unequivocal control accomplished through deeds of allocating (and withholding) resources, effective academic administration at this level largely resides in effective communication. What has so far been stressed, if not said in so many words, is that the dean or associate dean must become familiar with all facets of the departments he or she oversees. But the primary reason to have this knowledge is to be able to exercise influence on the directions departments take during the long periods between those relatively rare acts of allocation. And in that enterprise, the underlying condition for success is trust, in particular, faith in the clarity and honesty of communication—in both directions—between administration and department, via the channel of the chairperson.

How that chairperson is selected is therefore of particular importance and, insofar as possible, must be accomplished in a way that gives credibility to both directions of that two-way communication. We must now recall *Maxim 22*, with which this section began. Were election the mode of selection, those good departments would be likely to designate someone to lead them in the direction of becoming

[22] Over time, good departments get better, while bad departments get worse.

better; no such faith, on the other hand, is warranted where there is no track record of improvement. A procedure that is responsive to most actual situations is to have the dean solicit from each departmental member a confidential letter that discusses the chairpersonship of the department and includes as much detail and justification as the faculty member is willing to provide. When this approach is followed by face-to-face discussions with a few or many department members, the dean is likely to be well enough informed to identify his or her choice as the next chairperson. While formally the dean always appoints the chairperson, where the quality of the department warrants it, this procedure can be tantamount to election, by having the candidate of the majority appointed. In many other cases, the job will go to a candidate of a minority, with the dean adequately informed about the likely reception of that choice.

WHEN THINGS GO WRONG

The above points are not minor matters; these seemingly trifling concerns are as central as anything to the administration of an academic institution. For emphasis, I repeat in summary form. The primary purposes of the institution, for which all else exists, are carried out by faculty members, most of whom are grouped in departments. These faculty members possess the kind of autonomy, stressed from the outset, that makes them difficult to administer in any conventional sense, to harness them to the institution's purposes. Customary techniques all have their use—such as granting or withholding salary increases or perks and special privileges or their reduction—but they can be astonishingly ineffective in directing the efforts of faculty members to the purposes of the institution. Remember what *Maxim 3* says about the futility of *managing* faculty members!

[3] Academic administrators do not manage units composed of faculty or students, however much they may at times dream of doing so.

What matters more is to recognize and act upon the following principle: *Maxim 24. In administering an academic institution, act, whenever possible, to minimize the conflict between a faculty member's role as researcher and as teacher/educator.* The subtle and continuous influencing of the development of a department is important, both for its research and its pedagogic contributions to the institutional whole. No doubt deanly power and command over resources are among the necessary enabling conditions, but so are a dean who is deeply informed, whose messages in behalf of the institution are listened to because the messages from the department have been understood.

More drastic administrative measures to effect change are available and must, at times, be resorted to, even though the inertia expressed by *Maxim 22* is difficult to overcome. These measures are all variations on the theme that substitutes autocracy for departmental self-government. Instead of a chairperson who leads, for a term, a collective decision making process, a dean can appoint a head. Not only does

[22] Over time, good departments get better, while bad departments get worse.

the dean appoint such an administrator without consulting the flock that is to be ruled, but the head has no obligations beyond those of prudence to consult members of the department.

If headships are like monarchies—as contrasted with the republics of chairperson-led departments—a less permanent recourse to autocracy resembles colonial rule. Departments may temporarily be placed into "receivership" and governed neither by one of its own members nor by a faculty member of the department's discipline. Instead of going outside the institution to recruit a department head, an experienced faculty member in another, usually neighboring, discipline is enlisted to act as colonial administrator of the ailing department. In the absence of a suitable candidate for an unpleasant task, this custodial job might be performed by an associate dean or even by the dean.

In itself, the resort to autocracy can only bring about superficial changes. It might diminish strife by reducing the occasions when it can erupt; departmental procedures might be overhauled so as to be more suitable for the orderly conduct of business. However, if a department ails sufficiently to warrant resort to the kind of severe measures here sketched out, the only medicine that will effect a genuine cure is a change in the mix of its personnel. Other things being equal (and they aren't always), these structural modifications should be imposed only when budget or departmental demography support the anticipated departure of some and arrival of other faculty members. If a turnaround is highly unlikely without a change in faculty composition, know that such a renewal is difficult to bring off. Even heads are not exempt from the devastating effect of *Maxim 23*. What is more, it is never easy to attract good people into situations that, by definition, have significant unattractive features. Change comes slowly to academic institutions, even decline; it is thus difficult to bring about change for

[23] "A" people hire (or retain) "A" people, while "B" people hire "C" people.

the better. There is every motive in the world to prevent departments from deteriorating in the first place!

DEPARTMENTS AND MULTIDISCIPLINARY PROGRAMS

In all of the preceding, it was tacitly assumed that departments were brought into the world of academic institutions by the stork. It is time to say just enough to modify this myth, so as to introduce some comments on the organization of such complementary units as interdisciplinary and multidisciplinary programs, on changing a given departmental organization, and on the viability of alternatives to departmental organizations.

Different types of institutions are departmentalized in accord with different principles. At one end of a continuum is the world of arts and sciences, where the source of academic departments might be attributed two-thirds to the nature of the scholarly disciplines and one-third to the causal vagaries of history and sociology. In professional schools, this scheme is modified to varying degrees by the way work is organized in the domain of careers for which a given school prepares its students—differentially influenced, in other words, by what must be known by graduates seeking careers of different kinds.

If this summary is apt, some consequences follow immediately. To begin with, there is no point to searching for departmental boundaries in some Platonic realm of forms. For while disciplines are indeed individuated by a shared body of literature and common methods of investigation, they are at all times institutionally embodied and have their ever-moving histories. But how the professions are organized and the interaction between disciplines and professions change over time. What is studied within departments—aside from questions of range that are related to departmental size and where the boundaries between them lie is thus largely not a matter of ratiocination and planning, but a function of where and when the professorate was trained and of the ways in which the learned and other professions are organized.

An epistemologist might want to take a more cerebral tack when sorting out the disciplines. But useful for most administrative purposes is this positivist account that essentially identifies discipline and department. We have a need to characterize multidisciplinary research or teaching, and we do so by considering these to be enterprises that call for the collaboration of faculty members from several departments.

Most educational settings have various needs for such collaboration. Undergraduate education, particularly, does not always fit into the mold that is essentially shaped by graduate and professional training. There is a problem, however, about the creation of functioning units that work across departmental boundaries. The obstacles arise precisely out of the most desirable characteristics of successful departments—those that make them cohere as social and economic units.

Those natural centrifugal forces often make departments act as if they were city-states belonging to some loose confederation. Collaboration with members of other principalities, in such situations, can easily come to be regarded as disloyalty and the collaborator treated as an outcast. More frequent still is the effect of a department's cohesion as an economic unit. Teaching done in a multidisciplinary program is teaching *not* done for the department and is looked upon, therefore, as an unwarranted exportation of resources.

Administrative art must counteract those forces of nature, essentially in two connected and unsurprising ways. Because the landscape in which they must survive consists of departments, multidisciplinary programs must mimic their organization. This means, in the first place, leadership analogous to a departmental chairperson, in full possession of the dean's blessing. Because of the following maxim, a dean must make sure that the director of a multidisciplinary program is in a position to "purchase" the services of the departmental members needed to mount the program: *Maxim 25. To have status without a budget is to possess a gavel made of styrofoam.* Indeed, where budgets allow or where there is reason to make a particular effort to support a multidisciplinary program, it is appropriate to offer some extra inducement—called a bribe in other contexts—to the participant or department for such extra-departmental collaboration.

And yet, a clear distinction must be maintained between the creation and perpetuation of a multidisciplinary program and the founding of a new department. There certainly are occasions when the latter is justified—and we will shortly have a few words to say on that subject—but the essence of multidisciplinarity is the collaboration by persons who possess the skills and knowledge of their own different disciplines in the treatment of problems and issues in ways that could not be achieved by practitioners of a single discipline. Accordingly, constraints must be placed on the ways in which the director of a multidisciplinary program may deploy his or her budget. It should be usable to purchase the time of members of various departments and it might well serve to induce this or that department to engage a faculty member with knowledge and interests needed in the multidisciplinary program. At times, however, that may turn out to be difficult, not because of politically motivated foot dragging by a department, but because of a lack of excellent candidates. When that is so, the multidisciplinary program may be looking for someone trained in an area that is being replaced in its discipline by more recent developments. And when *that* is the case, the intellectual vitality of the multidisciplinary program itself must be questioned. All virtue is not automatically on the side of the multidisciplinary program. It should therefore be only rarely possible—under special circumstances that are well understood—for someone in a particular discipline to live wholly outside the departmental home of that discipline and risk the possibility of drifting out of touch with disciplinary progress and developments.

REORGANIZING DEPARTMENTS OR CREATING NEW ONES

The preceding discussion pointedly used the label, "multidisciplinary," rather than the more frequently employed "interdisciplinary." The meaning of the first term is reasonably clear: it characterizes some project that employs several disciplines. The latter is not equally perspicuous, because "inter" means "between," "among," or "in the midst of" and it is not immediately obvious just where that puts one in relation to two or more disciplines. To be between two stools is likely to find oneself lying on the ground; to be between day and night puts one either at dawn nor dusk, times that are a bit of both and neither. Let's reject the first of these models as too cynical, but derive a lesson from the second. As much as being *between* day and night, dawn and dusk are *different* from either, so it may be useful to use interdisciplinarity to point to the evolution of a new discipline out of components of older ones. At any rate, that is how, in retrospect, such fields as biochemistry or artificial intelligence got their start.

When such developments are vigorous and persistent, it may become necessary to create a new department or to reshape markedly the boundaries of existing ones. In either case, a group of faculty members will be changing departments and substituting old colleagues and environments for new, a change that some will be anxious to make and others will strongly resist. The magnitude of that wrench is alone sufficient to suggest a double caution regarding the introduction of major changes in departmental structure—not to mention long-run budgetary consequences. Only if two conditions obtain should an academic institution undertake a significant reorganization of its departmental structure. First, the envisaged future departmental configuration should correspond to changes in the affected disciplines, as that is exhibited in institutions in the forefront of those fields. If such major changes are made solely to accommodate *local* interests, the new configuration will either fail to endure for long or it will linger on in an intellectual backwater. Second, if the presence of adequate leadership is always a vital ingredient in the success of a department, that is doubly so where departments are new or have their nature significantly changed. Accordingly, moving forward with reorganizing is not advisable, unless satisfactory leadership of the newly configured departments is available.

ALTERNATIVES TO DEPARTMENTAL ORGANIZATION

This chapter assumes that departments are the standard academic units. That is not everywhere the case. First, some institutions are too small to bear departmentalization. Since it serves no useful purpose to have a collection of departments consisting of one or two persons each, faculty members must be grouped in broader units, assuming subdivisions to be appropriate in the first place. There is no all-purpose formula for such grouping, and none will work without some wrenches, not even the traditional arts and sciences tripartition into divisions of natural sciences, social sciences, and humanities. Second, some professional schools have no firm tradition of departmentalization. Some business schools, for example, are subdivided into departments, while many are not. And since, where no strong mores prevail, there is no reason to suppose that one model consistently fares better than the other, there are no *in principle* reasons to initiate change. We will see in the next chapter, however, that the presence or absence of subdivisions will bear on the way in which recommendations on faculty personnel are organized.

   A third reason for doing without conventional departments, is impatience with their insularity, even isolationism. Many a president, provost, or dean has fulminated at selfserving departments and their resistance to change or unwillingness to contribute to the academic commonweal. Although such sentiments are often understandable, it is mostly inadvisable to act on them. The stress, throughout this chapter, on the institutional embodiment of academic disciplines is not, I believe, misplaced. No doubt, there are things to be gained from the abandonment of a departmental structure—above all greater curricular flexibility and a stronger likelihood that more attention and imagination is expended on the general education of undergraduates.

But there are sacrifices to such an abandonment, as well. On the curricular side, pedagogy in the disciplines—in majors or concentrations, or at the graduate level—might lose something of its edge and fall behind recent developments. In some situations, this price may be worth paying for the sake of accomplishing a quite different set of educational goals. But giving up departments also has deeper consequences. For in the academic world as it actually exists, to be instructed in a discipline is to be socialized into a profession. This means that on the road to qualifying in an academic field, one acquires, as well, a set of habits and expectations peculiar to that discipline, certain ambitions vis-a-vis its journals, national societies, and so on. One of these expectations is that upon successful completion of one's training, one comes to work in a setting that fosters the ambitions conventionally associated with a field—that is, in academic departments, in areas that are customarily departmentalized.

If this "conservative" account of the workings of the academic world is correct, there will be many in it whose preference is to work in institutions that are organized as is customary. Accordingly, the pool from which the unconventionally organized institution will select its faculty will consist of those who are themselves to a degree idiosyncratic, plus those who are not in a position to be so exacting as to where they work. Over time, then, the institution that chooses to abandon the organizational scheme that is traditional for the professions it houses will also cultivate a faculty that will to a degree be eccentric.

André Gide was once asked who he thought was the greatest French poet. His reply, it is reported, was "Victor Hugo, élas." What we are confronting in this chapter may not be so different. It may well be true that the best organization of an academic institution is departmental, alas.

CHAPTER 7

Faculty Collaboration: Personnel and Educational Policy Decisions

PERSONNEL DECISIONS: INSTRUMENTAL GOALS AND THE REQUIREMENTS OF JUSTICE

The two types of action to be taken up in this chapter belong to the third, all-but determinative, category of decision making, where faculty members—often after having consulted students— make decisions, subject to administrative overruling only for strong reasons explicitly stated. These two—faculty personnel decisions and decisions regarding educational policy—are expressive of the collegial nature of academic institutions in precisely the way in which they are centrally distinct from corporations. Although many decisions are made by various faculty groups without administrators playing any role at all, especially within departments, most of these decisions concern "household" matters within allocated budgets or relatively local educational decisions made in conformity with preexisting institutional policies. By contrast, questions as to who shall be a member of the institution's faculty and at what rank and in what way students are to be educated stand at the center of the enterprise of any academic institution.

Moreover, the characterization of decision making as faculty action subject only to uncommon administrative veto does not do justice to the collaborative relationship between faculty and administration in these domains. We will take note of some of these connections as we go along, not only because they help explain what constitutes an appropriate justification of an administrative veto, but because these ramifications of faculty-administration collaboration shed further light on the organizational peculiarities of academic institutions.

There are many different types of faculty personnel decisions. There are decisions to hire faculty members in the first place; determinations to increase (or not) faculty members' salaries; decisions to retain faculty members (or not) when their contract period has come to an end; decisions to promote faculty members (or not) to the rank or status that confers a contract with indefinite tenure; determinations to promote faculty members (or not) to a higher rank, where a change in tenure status is not involved because the putative promotion comes either before the attainment of tenure or after. Collegiality requires faculty involvement in all these decisions, with some of them calling for student participation as well. Although we will take up the organization of only two types of personnel decision processes—hiring and promotion to tenure—it will be worthwhile to preface discussion with a general comment about two sets of criteria that function to some degree in all decisions about the fate of faculty members.

On the one hand, the object of personnel decisions is to *improve* the institution in which those decisions are made. Thus, when a salary is to be set or a promotion is under consideration, those making the decision seek to retain and encourage characteristics that are good for the institution and to eliminate or discourage undesirable traits. In that respect, colleges and universities are no different from the vast majority of enterprises in which employers aim to get the best work they can for the money they spend. On the other hand, it matters that the person whose fate is under consideration be treated *fairly*, both in the sense of getting what he or she deserves and in the sense of having his or her case dealt with in the same way in which other people are treated about whom analogous decisions are made. And while the requirement of fairness plays a role in many contexts in the United States at the end of the twentieth century, it is of particular importance in an academic setting with its central value of collegiality.

In principle, there need be no conflict between the pursuit of *instrumental* goals and the requirements of *justice*, to give each of these sets of desiderata a name. Whatever traits the institution may need for its successful functioning, it should be possible to determine conscientiously the degree of their presence in a candidate under consideration and it should be possible to treat each case in the same way as every other, so that no one is either unfairly favored or slighted.

But in practice there are tensions, a point readily illustrated with the aid of two types of competitions where judges are called upon to evaluate the performance of contestants. First, taken the job of determining the winner and subsequent order of the runners in a 1500 meter race. Controversies about the outcome of such competitions are rare because the task contestants are to perform has been clearly defined, the conditions under which they do their running have been standardized, the ways in which their performances are observed and measured are agreed upon and are supported by a suitable technology. If all the officials do their job competently, the spectators almost always go home satisfied that they know who won the race, came in second, third, and so on.

Consider, by contrast, the contest in which the quality of pianists is judged, where the object is to select as winner that person whose playing can be expected over time to evoke the greatest approval from the most discriminating and knowledgeable listeners, with the other contestants ranked in descending order behind that paragon. Judges in such a competition are not as fortunate as those of the runners. The traits they must judge are immensely complex and involve elements that permit considerable discretion, even subjectivity. While the conditions under which the contestants show what they can do can be somewhat standardized, the only technology that supports the work of the judges is their ears. Not surprisingly, controversies about piano competitions are normal and many observers fail to agree with the verdicts of the judges or with each other.

Now, it is a given what officials of foot races are to determine and what jurors of piano contests are to judge (more or less) and by what means. The complexity and variety of academic institutions, however, and the heterogeneous roles of faculty members make it less than obvious not merely *how* faculty members should be judged in various personnel decisions, but also just *which* traits should be singled out for evaluation.

Thus, because of that complexity and variety of academic institutions and the heterogeneous roles of faculty members, it becomes an important task for any institution's administration and faculty to decide just which characteristics and activities are of the greatest importance to them, so that it can be determined how they are to be evaluated, with a view to encouraging and rewarding them. But as such personnel policies are formulated and implemented, a tension between instrumental goals and the demands of justice may have a significant effect on those

policies and procedures themselves, with or without institutional awareness of that influence.

In an institution, for example, that might be described as imbued
with an entrepreneurial spirit—where "results" such as departmental
ratings and national recognition of faculty members are given dominant
weight—zeal might overcome the requirements of fairness. A person's
reputation as ascertained by phone calls to old friends in the field may
then be determinative in various personnel decisions. The way one case
is considered might be different from how another is handled and the
subjectivity of informants may play a dominant role in any one of them.
Whoever is responsible for making institutional policy is here willing,
inadvertently or deliberately, to have the requirements of justice—
rewarding or punishing in accord with what is deserved and treating like
cases in a like manner—give way to the demands of attaining instrumental goals.

In another situation, the demands of justice may be paramount for
personnel decisions. Where that is so, those who formulate and implement personnel policies will be strongly motivated to evaluate faculty
traits that can be easily detected and compared. In extreme cases, the
notion of merit in any sense may be tossed out of the window altogether,
on the grounds that what is meritorious and to what degree is essentially
subjective and immeasurable, leaving the measurable length of time
served as the central or even sole characteristic considered in important
personnel decisions. The underlying principle is this: the simpler the
criteria and the more easily discerned who possesses more and less of the
relevant attributes, the easier it is to be fair and to be seen to be fair by
candidates and onlookers.

APPOINTMENT

By exaggerating, I have tried to make vivid this tension between instrumental goals and the requirements of justice because every college and
university must devise a personnel system that effectively considers
substantive criteria that are significant for the institution's welfare and
renders its judgments fairly. The history of such institutions suggests
that this is unlikely to happen where such outcome is not an explicit aim
of policy makers.

Clearly, the quality of personnel decisions is not just a function of
how those who make them are organized. In an important sense, who

the people are (remember *Maxim 23*) and what procedures they use makes a bigger difference to the outcome. Just as honest and competent people must be organized into a court system, where they

[23] "A" people hire (or retain) "A" people, while "B" people hire "C" people.

play designated roles as judges, jury members, opposing lawyers, if they are to make *legal* judgments, so good and well-intentioned people need to be appropriately organized to render acceptable personnel decisions.

The first type of decision to be taken up—hiring faculty members—is a crucially important one because, in the vast majority of colleges and universities, who is hired has a more significant impact on what kind of faculty an institution has than all other decisions put together. First, there is the matter of scope. All other procedures consider only people who are already at the institution, while the net cast by those who are hiring is indefinitely large. The range of possibilities is immeasurably greater. But the second reason stems from the duality of desiderata in all personnel decisions, the instrumental requirements and those of justice. When we compare hiring decisions, on one side, with contract renewal and tenure decisions, on the other, we see the requirement of justice has different consequences. In the former, fairness—to a degree embodied in laws that govern hiring procedures—essentially demands that we not discriminate among candidates in ways that are irrelevant to the tasks the person will be required to perform.

This procedure usually leaves a world of people to be considered and a myriad of relevant skills and characteristics. Some candidates are eliminated quickly; others, who *prima facie* meet the institution's needs more adequately, are investigated more thoroughly. *Some* consideration is owed to all who apply, but not *equal* consideration. The work done to find out what candidates can do aims at making the best possible appointment; meticulousness is not due to all candidates as it is to all colleagues. The requirements of justice, here, will be seen to be less complex than when colleagues are considered for tenure or promotion and are therefore less likely to defeat the pursuit of instrumental goals.

To help assure that the best possible appointment is actually made—and the requirements of justice fulfilled—the labors of faculty, students, and administrators must be appropriately deployed. To begin, the existence of the opening (here assumed not to involve tenure) and the substantive way in which it is described must be the product of the kind of dean-chairperson discussions stressed in the previous chapter. The future shape of an institution is importantly determined by such definitions. Will the opening bolster a subfield already represented or take the institution into new areas. Is the person needed more for undergraduate (or basic professional) teaching or for the conduct and supervision of research? Even though there may be no perfectly suitable candidates and even though any selection process is fallible, aims must be clearly known and defined. The goal of a faculty search constitutes one corner of the vision of the institution's future.

Success in the execution of a search is made more likely by a kind of vertical division of labor. On the "bottom" is the departmental search committee that has the responsibility for generating and working through applications, including the assessment of the work of the more plausible candidates and including off-campus interviews where feasible. Where participation in multidisciplinary teaching or research will be wanted of the successful candidate, a dean is well advised to appoint a faculty member from a second relevant discipline to the search committee—for his or her voice, if not necessarily to vote.

The next step on the ladder is the consideration of a short list of candidates by an entire department. The department issues requests to the dean to have candidates visit for multiple interviews and such "performances" as teaching a class, conducting a seminar, or delivering a lecture reporting research results. The voice of students regarding a prospective faculty member is appropriately heard at this point. A student committee—after consulting fellow students—should be asked to provide its views on all aspects of a candidate's potential faculty role about which they feel qualified to judge. The scope of such judgments will depend on the nature of the field and how advanced these students are in their studies, but it will presumably always include an assessment of the candidate as teacher, advisor, and mentor from a perspective that is fundamentally different from that of faculty members essaying similar assessments.

When the interviewing process is concluded, the department (not the search committee), through its chairperson, recommends to the dean that an offer be made to a candidate.

The dean or associate dean, through the approval of campus visits and, finally, of an offer, is above all in the business of quality control. The dean is a monitor who makes sure that the laws and policies designed to satisfy the requirements of justice are observed. But that officer has a substantive role as well. An important operational instantiation of *Maxim 23* can be stated in a new maxim: *Maxim 26. The best is the enemy of the good.* The interpretation here of this two-edged

[23] *"A" people hire (or retain) "A" people, while "B" people hire "C" people.*

precept points to cases where fear of leaner futures may lead departments to judge the *best* candidate generated by the search process to be acceptable without facing up to the question as to whether or not that candidate is actually *good*. It can happen that not a single candidate for a given job—or none willing to accept an offer—meets a certain standard, either because none is out there that year, or because the search was poorly conducted, or because there was competition from more powerful institutions. Then the best available may not be good enough, and it becomes the dean's dual job to provide the assurance that virtue will not be punished—that the unwillingness to compromise standards will not cost the department its position—and to be sufficiently informed about candidates to know when a departmental recommendation was *merely* a recommendation for the best. In the absence of such *self*-restraint, the dean must do the restraining and turn the recommendation down. And in conformity with the type of decision making under discussion, the dean must provide an explanation for the veto issued.

Dean and department thus collaborate in making faculty appointments. The provost must, as was insisted upon in Chapter 4, remain "above" this appointment process. Besides exercising leadership in the *formulation* of faculty appointment policies for the institution, that chief academic officer must oversee their implementation and, equally important, ascertain on an ongoing basis the degree to which institutional practices and administrators are achieving the goals these policies were designed to bring about. In this age of sophisticated bureaucratization, the check on *conformity* with policies is likely to be accomplished by staff use of formal "checking" procedures. As was suggested earlier, the latter, substantive job is best accomplished by asking deans periodically to give an account as to how the appointments they have approved have improved their departments and schools or why they failed to do so.

CONFERRAL OF TENURE

The appointment decision that considers the conferral of tenure (usually but not always accompanied by a promotion) has the most formidable justice requirements. This time—as in all other remaining types of decisions—the persons about whom judgments are made are members of the institution that is governed by principles of collegiality. As was the case in recruitment, all are entitled to be treated by a process that considers only those characteristics that are relevant to the institutional roles played (rather than those singled out by whim or prejudice and of no consequence for the performance of the tasks required). In these cases, however, every candidate is entitled to be treated in the same way as every other and the need is considerably heightened for conscientious implementation of the procedures devised in conformity with these requirements.

This need leads us to another maxim: *Maxim 27. The obligations of conscientiousness are relative to the moral importance of the task to be accomplished.* I am required, for example, to make a much greater effort to overcome obstacles in order to be prompt if I promised to serve as your witness in a legal proceeding than if I promised to meet you for lunch. Of all the remaining regular personnel decisions, that concerning tenure is the weightiest. It determines whether the candidate will or will not retain his or her job, and it settles whether the institution will or will not have an employee for a term that will end only when the employee decides to leave or retire (or dies). The institution can dismiss only by using an elaborate procedure showing cause. The tenure decision decides whether the students and faculty of a department retain a teacher and colleague they may have loved or hated for more than half a decade. Even though I maintain that at most colleges and universities the hiring decision has a more powerful effect on the shape of the institution over time, the combination of instrumental requirements and the demands of justice permit no other regular personnel decision to compete in gravity with the tenure decision.

For the tenure decision, there must be a structure that makes maximal conscientiousness likely: one that brings together advocacy, substantive expertise, and the kind of awareness, institutional and procedural, that assures objectivity. In practice, this calls for three layers in the decision making process: a department that puts forward the case for conferral of tenure; a committee of three or so scholars from cognate fields (or from the same field, if from outside the institution); and a committee that is representative and so constituted as to be seen as representative of the entire unit or institution. Maxim 13, which pits representativeness against effectiveness, suggests the need to keep the committee's size at not much more than a dozen.

[13] *As a committee increases in size, its capacity to be representative becomes greater, while its potentiality for effectiveness decreases.*

The job of the department in a grant of tenure is advocacy, putting forward the best case for the candidate. (If that best case is not persuasive or seriously qualified, subsequent examiners of the dossier are likely to conclude that the departmental decision itself was half-hearted.) The task of what is usually referred to as the *ad hoc* committee is to evaluate the substance of the case. Depending on the field, it may be possible for such a group to make a direct assessment of the candidate's work; more often than not, it is limited to the appraisal of secondary evidence in the form of letters from outsiders in the candidate's field, from reviews, citation indices, teaching evaluations, and the like. The process relies on the relatedness of the fields of the members of the committee to that of the candidate for familiarity with the standards and mores that prevail in the candidate's domain.

The broad committee that considers all the cases has a different job. It, like the dean, is in two ways in the business of quality control, exercising its function both in behalf of the institution and in behalf of the peers whose cases come before it. One part of that is substantive: the committee represents the standards of the institution, vis-a-vis the standards of various departments and disparate *ad hoc* committees. The second aspect is procedural, with the committee required to ascertain whether every case has been considered with the requisite thoroughness and fairness—and to see that appropriate steps are taken when flaws are discovered in the consideration of a candidate.

The job such a tenure committee performs lies somewhere between the role assigned to juries and judges. Its members must be able to assess the evidence placed before it, evidence that is disparate not only because it originates in different scholarly domains, but because it takes such varied form. The content of testimonial letters needs to be assessed, but also the importance and relevance of the writers; the magnitude of a record of publications matters, but also its significance. No field-expertise is called for, but the ability to evaluate expert evidence given by others. In no way can a committee appraise the truth of statements made by the experts, but they can gauge their credibility. Like judge and jury, such a group of peers is capable of reaching a conclusion in cases of different kinds by virtue of knowledge of the world—here the specifically academic world—and by virtue of a willingness and ability to be meticulous in carrying out the assignment given.

But note that judge and jury are not asked to make sense of some chunk of the world as it flows by in its complex irregularity. Just as trials are structures designed to bring order to that stream, in conformity with pertinent canons of relevance, so tenure committees are confronted with formally composed dossiers, rather than with people ceaselessly engaged in activity. And this comment points to an obligation of the dean as administrator of the promotions process, the proficient discharge of which is indispensable for the effectiveness of the entire venture. A thoughtful "definition" must be created as to what is to be included in a properly composed promotions dossier and all parties who are asked to contribute to it must be informed of these requirements. And since the academic world is no different from any other, where some people do and others don't perform the tasks assigned to them with skill and conscientiousness, a monitoring system must be created to see that what should happen actually does.

The system here sketched out recommends to the dean to promote or not. If it functions well, the dean, with infrequent exceptions, will agree with that counsel. A dean's occasional rejection of a tenure committee's advice must, by the principles we have formulated, be supported by an explanation to the recommending body.

Frequent disagreements, on the other hand, can be the symptom of a variety of ailments. Perhaps the recommending system just described is not functioning well and "needs fixed," as Pittsburgh grammar would put it, either in its form or in the individuals selected to participate in it. A second alternative is that the faculty and the dean are not applying the same standards to the tenure cases they are considering. In that case, the dean must find additional ways—besides repeatedly saying "no"—to communicate what standard of evaluation he or she expects the faculty to employ. The modification of ways in which faculty are evaluated is an important way of changing an institution and, as we will take up below in the "Postscript on Change," a function most likely initiated by administrators.

A final alternative is that the dean is not doing a good job. And this is where provost or president comes in. Since the charters of most institutions do not permit anyone other than the chief executive officer or the board to grant contracts with indefinite tenure, the dean's conclusion will have to take the form of a recommendation to the provost, if there is one, or to the president, if there is not. As was discussed in Chapter 4, the normal job of that top supervisory level is, again, scrutiny as to the conformity of the dean's promotion recommendations with institutional policies, with rejections of recommendations rare and mostly traceable to some special set of circumstances. However, the provost (or president) must pay careful heed to *each* promotions dossier in its entirety, including the coherence of the final recommendation with the rest, and to *all* the dossiers generated over a period of time. Much useful evidence will be contained in these massive stacks of paper about the quality of the performance of a dean.

One further conclusion with policy implications, previously asserted and discussed, is made more intelligible by the perusal of such material: assuming it to be a significant instrumental goal to maximize the quality of an institution's faculty, the hiring decision is the most telling. Tenure dossiers will show that this decision introduces a distinct element of caution into the substantive evaluation of faculty members, one that is not present to that degree in the assessment of outside applicants in the course of the hiring process. Moreover, the fact that in tenure proceedings one's own colleagues are being individually evaluated—in contrast with the appraisal of considerable numbers of unknown aspirants— introduces a propensity to give candidates for tenure a benefit of the doubt that is not accorded to outsiders. Since the demands of justice require the first of these differences and civility calls for the second, it would neither be easy nor desirable to get rid of them. Perhaps differences such as these underlie the practice at a small number of elite institutions to make the hiring and the tenure decision identical, by simply not "promoting" colleagues to a tenured rank. In any case, these comparisons should induce one to develop mechanisms that make it likely that both types of decisions are made with the greatest care.

EDUCATIONAL POLICY

A *Compleat Prymer* would now continue with discussions of several other faculty personnel decisions. This briefer version will ask the reader to infer from what has been said to analogous modes of faculty-administration collaboration in other such areas, while we continue on to consider mechanisms for the formulation of educational policy. Although this task also belongs to the all-but determinative decision category that allows for infrequent administrative vetoes, there are important differences in the structure of the faculty-administration collaboration.

In an important sense, educational policy is the corporate faculty's domain in a way in which nothing else is. This is most obvious at the level of particular fields of study. Within two sets of limits, departments and programs set the requirements for the students that concentrate in their fields and determine what instruction to make available to nonspecialists. Only one of these checks can be taken to be a genre of administrative veto. A department cannot require students to take a course in a subject which no existing faculty member can teach, nor insist that 400 students take a laboratory course when its facilities can only handle 100.

[8] *Few significant campus de-*
cisions are without budgetary
implications.

As an application of *Maxim 8*—which proclaims the ubiquity of budgetary implications—administrative action or inaction affects the curriculum via an essentially fiscal channel, while disagreements on educational policy largely remain moot.

The second type of constraint placed on the educational practices of a department or program are the requirements, restrictions, and policies that are not administrative, but stem from the actions of faculty committees above the departmental and programmatic level. We must turn, then, to consider the ways of formulating educational policies for an entire school or institution.

A number of reasons make this a more complex task than one might think, not the least of them the truth of *Maxim 1*, affirming the natural centrifugality of academic institutions. In view of

[1] *In academic institutions, the*
forces of nature *are centrifugal;*
organizational art *must be used*
to create propensities toward co-
herence.

this decentralization, broadly representative school-wide or institution-wide educational policies committees tend to evince a live-and-let-live attitude and stand as little as possible in the way of the will of the departments or whatever the component units are. A dominant concern of such groups is likely to be the maintenance of a level playing field, a consideration that leads to the specification of a maximum number of courses for the major, for example, while following a permissive and even-handed policy for the approval of new course offerings. Where such a committee is asked to deal with the courses that students are required to take outside their concentrations one can count on an "equitable" distribution of such requirements.

There is a place for such a minimalist, care-taking, traffic managing educational policy or curriculum committee and, following the advice of *Maxim 12*, it is appropriately composed of members who are representa-

[12] *Choosing the members of a*
committee in a way appropriate
to its function is likely to increase
the effectiveness of its operation.

tive of the constituent departments or units and elected by the faculty. To have a slate of candidates prepared by a committee on committees will increase the likelihood that committee members actually have an interest in educational policy, but it will not change its basically *laisser aller* character. The administrative role vis-a-vis this committee, usually in the person of an associate dean, is to be both fuel and engine by providing the staff (read "paper") work and keeping the group harnessed to its tasks. Administrative limits to the committee's educational policy making, if any, are again likely to have a fiscal origin, such as not permitting course offerings substantially in excess of a department's capacity to deliver them within a given span of time.

Such a housekeeping curricular committee does not so much restrain centrifugal forces as keep them in order. It does little, therefore, to contribute to the conversion of a collection of professors-of-a-variety-of-disciplines into a corporate establishment concerned with the education of students. The art that counteracts and channels into a single direction begins with the administrative leadership that formulates an educational problem to be solved and sets an instructional task for the faculty-as-a-community-of-educators to accomplish.

At the beginning, then, is not the deed, but the thought and that thought, however much dependent on the reflections of many, must ultimately come to be situated in the mind of a single person capable of taking action. On the advice of *Maxim 11*, reflection and its distillation are best accomplished by a committee that is especially formed to carry out the proposed mission.

[11] Committees whose mission is to perform routine and ongoing functions are ill suited for tasks that require them to move outside the framework within which they normally operate.

The range of such possible missions is large. Concerns about the education of undergraduates are the most familiar. What distribution requirements should be set (or how should a current set of such requirements be modified)? What courses, if any, should be taken by *all* students? What courses should be especially created (or modified) to contribute to the general education of students? What knowledge should students have before they are permitted to graduate; what skills should they have mastered before they are awarded their degrees? These are among the many questions on which special committees are asked to make recommendations to a faculty with the aim of implicating an *entire* faculty in the education of *each* student.

While it is generally conceded that the concerns of undergraduate education go beyond the aegis of individual departments, even if the implementation of that judgment is mostly half-hearted, not even much lip service is paid, in graduate and professional instruction, to the thesis that there might be educational issues that transcend the interests of the several disciplines. Accordingly, representative maintenance committees are prevalent at the graduate level, serving as necessary keepers of minimal rules, while department-transcending missions tend to remain unformulated. Here, if anywhere, it must be clear that the impetus for the consideration of broader issues in advanced education can only come from an administrator, such as a graduate dean, who is to a degree freed from the bonds of departmental loyalty. And the fact that such concerns are only seldom framed as tasks to be performed is much more testimony to the power of those centrifugal forces than to the paucity of missions to be accomplished. In any case, where serious educational questions are raised about graduate and professional programs, it is *a fortiori* imperative to create a special committee for the purpose.

What kind of committee should be formed and what relation should it have to the faculty as a whole? For reasons already stated, a committee elected and designed to be representative is unlikely to be imagina-

[12] Choosing the members of a committee in a way appropriate to its function is likely to increase the effectiveness of its operation.

tive and daring in its solution to problems. In conformity with Maxim 12, a dean will therefore want to use a mechanism that is capable of selecting faculty members who have a genuine interest in the issues to be taken up. Further, while Maxim

[13] As a committee increases in size, its capacity to be representative becomes greater, while its potentiality for effectiveness decreases.

13 reminds us that effectiveness requires the committee to be kept compact, it is nevertheless appropriate for students to be represented to contribute their own unique perspective on their education to the deliberations. Moreover, if only because of the likelihood of budgetary implications of substantive curricular changes—remember Maxim 8!—such a group should be joined by a member from the office of the dean to keep open committee-administration lines of communication. Finally, it is crucial

[8] Few significant campus decisions are without budgetary implications.

to include some members who possess particular credibility and persuasiveness vis-a-vis the rest of the faculty, a practice that can more than compensate for a lack of representativeness. For unless both of the following goals are accomplished, the venture of educational reform will have failed. First, the report must be of a quality to recommend actions that are significant *improvements* over current practice, and second, it must be *adopted* by the faculty, at least for the most part.

As can be inferred from the discussion in Chapter 2, institutions of different size and complexity will have to use different ways to move from a special committee report to faculty legislation. But whatever the road—from immediate discussion and vote by a senate or full faculty to the use of intermediate councils—the dean must retain full awareness of the fact that any report proposing to establish educational policies and practices for an entire school or institution is pitted against those centrifugal forces. And if it takes art to combat them, it also takes money. As artist-in-chief, the dean must support worthwhile educational goals not only with deanly powers of persuasion, but also with the deanly budget.

CHAPTER 8

Faculty Collaboration: The Juridical Role

SOME INSTITUTIONAL CONDITIONS

We turn now to another kind of faculty-administration collaboration, where the decisions are juridical. Again, the decision category is all-but determinative, with the faculty judgment administratively overruled only for strong reasons explicitly stated. Our concern, then, is with faculty juridical mechanisms designed to recommend on grievances by faculty members, to hear faculty appeals from adverse personnel decisions, and to make judgments concerning contentions by an administration that a faculty member has engaged in improper conduct sufficiently serious to merit some punitive action, including dismissal. While methods for accomplishing these objectives may to some degree resemble grievance procedures in governmental and business establishments (the latter especially where they are regulated by a union contract), as well as partially mimic the workings of law in secular society, they nevertheless retain features that are peculiar to the academic world.

The object of any juridical process is to make equitable judgments in the particular cases that arise in an institution. Except for luck, nothing makes these jobs easy. Four conditions must be met if a satisfactory outcome is to be the norm for an institution. First, a mechanism must be established that harnesses people to this juridical task in an appropriate manner. Second, the persons deployed to deal with individual cases must have suitable procedures to follow. Third, the institution must possess a compilation of precepts that serve as guides for making individual judgments. One can distinguish two types of such precepts. One is a set of general and abstract beliefs and declarations about the nature of the institution, while the other is a set of specific rules and regulations governing behavior in a variety of contexts and situations. The first set might be formulated as the preamble of a governance statement or even be a part of an institution's charter. The second set is typically found in faculty handbooks, documents articulating research policy, and the like. The fourth condition for smooth functioning of campus juridical processes is an accepted way of thinking and acting in the institution, a set of traditions, an ethos. While many of these beliefs and practices will be borrowed from conceptions of proper behavior in the "outside" world, some are peculiar to the academy and to the particular institution in question.

With respect to the fourth of these requirements, not much can specifically be done to establish it. An ethos and traditions are created in ways analogous to the explanation given as to how Cambridge University came to have such beautiful lawns: "Throw some seed into the ground and roll for a few hundred years." Such confessions of ineffectualness should nevertheless be modified by the observation that numerous daily actions, especially by those in leadership roles, do contribute to the formation of an ethos, even though the slowness of development may make that fact invisible to the actors.

Considerably more is to be said about the compilation of general precepts needed to deal with individual cases. Let's begin with the mundane but vitally necessary, the myriad of rules to be found in every college and university about what to do and what not to do. Let's call these rules behavioral regulations. Then there are directives about processes to be followed—call these procedural rules—in the pursuit of various decisions, sometimes by individuals, usually by groups or committees. While in this context, the most important desideratum is that such rules should be written with clarity and precision, something not always easy to do. Revulsion against sexual harassment is widespread, but it is hard to convert these feelings into an explicit code that clearly specifies what is unacceptable behavior. This code is needed to apprise faculty and staff of what is proscribed and provide administrators with criteria by which to identify putative transgressions. Research integrity has become a national concern. Yet it is by no means easy to formulate guidelines that cut across numerous disciplines and ways of conducting research. Clarity in the formulation of procedures, such as those to be used in making various personnel decisions, is at least as important. Conscientious departments or promotions committees should not be in a quandary as to what they are to do. Nor should a panel assessing a claim to a procedural violation be puzzled as to just what procedures *should* have been followed.

Many of these tasks of formulation are difficult and often performed poorly. Still, doing better "merely" requires that there be the will—not a stipulation to be taken for granted—considerable patience, and the political and administrative ability to deploy a certain amount of analytic and technical skill in the execution of this assignment. But the framing of those broader principles raises deeper questions, for their delineation contributes to the very definition of the institution and provides the setting within which all specific regulations and procedures are interpreted. The less developed an institution's traditions, the greater the need for broad, "constitutional" statements.

One set of principles pertains to academic freedom. The easy part is the necessary assertion that the institution subscribes to the principles of academic freedom and thus neither prescribes nor proscribes what may be taught or investigated. Often this "traditional" *Lehrfreiheit*— though not a tradition known for its wide distribution around the globe nor for the length of its history at any one location—is formulated in unconditional terms: what goes on in the classroom is solely the concern of the teacher; what views are expressed in research reports from laboratory or library is solely the business of the inquirer. But absolute formulations are misleading. One obvious limitation to this freedom can here be ignored, call it the "real world" constraint, sometimes reasonable, sometimes deplorable: students vote with their feet; agencies support this research project but not that; publishers accept one manuscript but not another.

Two other kinds of qualifications cannot be overlooked. The easier of the two pertains to a limitation that springs from the professor's role as educator. Students are not merely enrolled in courses, but in programs that aim, as a *whole*, to achieve some pedagogic purpose. But if so, that entirety will to a degree have to determine the character of the parts, an abstract locution that translates into the mundane observation that the needs of a program partially dictate the content of particular component courses and therein curtail the freedom of an instructor to decide what and what not to teach. In short, it must be stated or implied that the freedom to teach is not so absolute as to stand in the way of the achievement of educational goals that go beyond the individual instructor's classes.

While this first limitation is insufficiently recognized—to the detriment of the education of hosts of students—it is less likely to raise as deep a set of problems as a second kind. Presumably, it is assumed—where, as is usual, there is no explicit statement—that the person who enjoys that *Lehrfreiheit* professes his or her discipline *competently*. And competence—again "presumably"—is determined by the community of practitioners of the field, within and outside a given institution. But of course, the line is not at all clear between innovativeness or mere eccentricity, on the one hand, and incompetence, on the other, making the academy understandably squeamish about rushing into judgments of incompetence. (After all, tenure was originally invented to protect young turks from the old guard, who were not above using dismissal to defend their way of doing things.) Undoubtedly, students suffer at times from the academy's diffidence about tackling the problem of incompetent teachers and it has certainly generated some flamboyant public cases, such as professorial espousals of dubious racial theories. But, given the professionalism—not to say conventionalism—of the vast majority of American academic institutions, the disinclination to make explicit that competence as a condition for the enjoyment of academic freedom may have been wise protection from external interference in the affairs of colleges and universities.

In the near future, however, the issue of competence may be raised in a somewhat different way and with a frequency that will not permit it to be ignored. In the absence of all mandatory retirement, only two causes, besides death, will lead faculty members to vacate their positions. Either the professor decides to retire, with or without special inducements, or the institution "decides" that the faculty member can no longer do the job. But the institution's "decision" is of a radically different sort from the faculty member's. The first is freely taken, whether as a result of deep thought or whim. The latter must be the product of a procedure that *establishes* that the faculty member is unable to do what he or she is being paid to do.

When the impairment is physical and, say, a stroke prevents a faculty member either from meeting with his or her students or from speaking to them, the case for forcible retirement has presumably been made. I say "presumably," because someone might make the case that the infirmities of old age are "handicaps" that should not be discriminated against.

If so, there will certainly be problems for academic (and other) institutions, though such issues of physical health do not themselves raise questions of academic freedom.

But the effect of the deterioration of mental health certainly does raise such questions. Since modern medicine seems to have been more successful in staving off the decline of physical vigor than of mental functioning, we can expect an increasing number of cases where attempts are made, or should be made, to require a faculty member to retire from teaching or research because of failing competence. In the future, it will have to be explicit that academic freedom and, especially, *Lehrfreiheit* is a right enjoyed only by the competent. That this clearly calls for a process of peer judgment is a topic developed below.

A central purpose of the "constitutional" matters we have been discussing is to sketch a boundary indicating the region of the permitted in a given academic institution. While the emphasis in such talk is on what is allowed—so that citizens of the academy feel free to roam in their studying, investigating, and teaching—that coin clearly has another side. Our discussion of the relationship of competence to academic freedom has shown that straying into the territory outside that border can have consequences, including total banishment. But there is another kind of freedom pertaining to the academy that deserves embodiment in an institution's traditions or statements of fundamental principles, one concerned with the relationship to the institution of transgressions by its members of various laws of the land.

To explain this relationship, a distinction between what might be called "academic malfeasance" and "secular malfeasance" is helpful, with plagiarism or giving a student a passing grade in response to a bribe being examples of the first and reckless driving or shoplifting examples of the second. The principle is simple, although it requires some explanation to prevent misunderstandings. One might think of the operation of a division of labor. Civil authorities do not get involved in the administration of the "laws" of the academy, while academic institutions are not the administrators of civil law and do not have the job of prosecuting transgressors and punishing them. The academy's judicial and disciplining activity should be limited to the kinds of actions that can be shown to undermine such central academic functions as teaching and research—granting that this rubric is not without its ambiguities. It is therefore appropriate for a college to prosecute a faculty member for falsifying laboratory reports for use in teaching or in publications. It is not appropriate for that college to discipline a faculty member for stealing T-shirts from the book store; that's the job of the town's police.

However, nothing prevents *both* domains from declaring the *same* action to be a crime. Town and gown might each legislate against sexual harassment, the latter perhaps because such acts disrupt the proper functioning of the academic institution. Both university and state might proscribe plagiarizing, the latter because it regards using the words of another as a form of theft. Furthermore, the academy in no way constitutes a special sanctuary from civil law; its members have the normal obligations of citizenship with respect to cooperation with civil authorities about violations of civil laws. If the police suspect a professor of breaking and entering somewhere off campus, the college faculty and administrators have the same rights and obligations about assisting civil authorities in pursuit of their suspect as any other citizen.

These principles help in two ways to protect the academy from certain intrusions, especially during politically turbulent times. If the town considers it trespassing to demonstrate against the building of a nuclear plant and a professor is arrested for doing so, this should have no consequences for that faculty member's role on campus. The maintenance of the principles being enunciated here, would have saved the jobs of those faculty members who were held in contempt of Congress for not "naming names" to the House Unamerican Activities Committee. A person's relationship to the state would not *ipso facto* determine his or her relationship to the academy and in this way shelter the academy somewhat from incursions by the state.

(The reciprocal of this relationship is, strictly speaking, not relevant in this context, but worth mentioning for the sake of symmetry. Breaches of the rules of an academic institution are the concern of its administration, the keepers, so to speak, of those rules. Other things being equal, the enforcement of the institution's regulations and the disciplining of transgressors is the institution's responsibility. Other things are *not* equal only when an authorized college or university official finds that help is needed from outside the institution to preserve the safety of its members. Until the judgment of need is made *inside* the institution, it remains inappropriate for civil authorities to intrude.)

THE JURIDICAL PROCESS

We are ready, finally, to discuss the mechanism by which the several types of juridical functions are appropriately handled. These functions are making judgments regarding grievances, appeals, and administration claims of the appropriateness of disciplining a faculty member. A close analogue to those who perform them is the jury, as it might function if there were neither judge nor lawyers. The object being fairness and impartiality, such judgments must be made by peers who represent the community but have no personal connection with or interest in the case on which they are recommending. When the system works as it should, the recommendations that are made are accepted as credible by the entire institution, even if it is too much to expect that the person who is found against will be happy with the outcome.

But what is about to be described is a formal process in which the institution and the individual who is pitted against it invest considerable time, energy, and psychic (or institutional) wear and tear. An ombuds-man—who is free to work *informally*, proposes compromises and even effects deals that bend rules in ways in which no formal juridical process can—is in a position to reduce markedly the need for the much more elaborate and less flexible procedure.

In Chapter 2, we stressed that the method by which a group of persons is selected to engage in these juridical functions must be most sensitive to the importance of *fairness* as a central value. What matters is that those dealing with any particular case be chosen from a panel of peers of the grieving or accused individual, a panel that might be elected, without intervention of a committee on committees or nomi-nating committee, or chosen by lot from the entire roster of peers. However, a juridical process cannot be expected to function either effectively or appropriately without leadership, an undertaking that consists of several components that are often overlooked. To fulfill these functions, the faculty must also elect a steering committee of three experienced elders, most sensibly from a slate carefully put together by a committee on committees.

The first function of the steering committee is to make a *prima facie* judgment at the outset that there is a case to be investigated. Their preliminary scrutiny of the charge and the evidence brought forward to support it must show that the grievance is real or the transgression nontrivial, that there may indeed have been discrimination or a proce-dural violation in a promotions or tenure case. (The juridical system is not designed to make academic judgments. If a faculty member believes that a dean has made the wrong judgment about the worth of his or her scholarship, he surely has the right to ask that the person to whom the dean reports overrule the dean on substantive grounds. The juridical process can consider only claims that the *way* the judgment was made was faulty; and if this turns out to be the case, the judgment-making process, not the juridical one, must try again.)

The second task of the steering committee is to attempt mediation, to propose a compromise acceptable to both sides of the dispute. Even where an ombudsman has had a chance to make the attempt to mediate, the possibility that a steering committee might succeed cannot be ruled out. Each level passed without successful mediation brings closer the level at which a resolution is imposed. Thus, the steering committee will go to the panel and select an investigating committee only when the attempt to adjudicate fails. It will do so, taking into consideration the need to have an impartial group, both with respect to the individuals who are picked and the aggregate that is composed. Both sides should have the right to put forward reasons why some proposed group member should not serve in the case, though the last word must belong to the steering committee, which also designates the chairperson of the investigative committee.

The final vital cluster of jobs of the steering committee is often overlooked. The committee—or one of its members—must be ready to advise each investigative committee on how to proceed; serve as liaison, where needed, to relevant administrative offices and faculty groups; and monitor the investigation's progress. Faculty members are not born with the know-how needed for this most unacademic function, or the requisite assertiveness for obtaining documents or testimony from high level administrators, or the diligence to keep them on the job in such a way as to procure swift justice. The members of the steering committee must be a help in all these ways, as well as a prod.

The actual task of an investigative committee is to go through the relevant documents and interview all the persons the group believes can shed light on the case. Its method must be informal and take the form of an inquiry. A committee must not fall into the trap of trying to mimic the adversarial model of a common law trial; such a technique is dependent on trained advocates, on detailed rules of procedure and evidence, and on an overseeing judge, none of which is available in our setting.

The most drastic kind of case that an investigative committee can be asked to consider is the termination of a faculty contract of indefinite tenure (usually shortened to "removal from tenure") for cause, usually labelled "unprofessional conduct." Whether that conduct is a product of incompetence or is rooted in a particular action or activity, these extreme cases are especially helped by well-executed "constitutional" statements earlier taken up, together with an ethos that encompasses the entire institution. Such cases not only have serious consequences for the people directly involved, but the impact of just one of them on an entire institution can be deep and lasting. The judiciousness and credibility of the investigating committee can do much to mitigate shocks to the social fabric.

Credibility is in part rooted in the quality of the report with which an investigation concludes. The task is completed with a finding in the case, communicated both to the appropriate administrator and to the person whose case is under consideration. Since the committee plays a role in collaborative decision making without power to act on its conclusions, its effectiveness depends importantly on its persuasiveness. Committees are well advised to realize that their audience has not had the experience they have recently traversed. Accordingly, their conclusion must be supported by the reasons that led to its adoption, with finding and reasons embedded in a summary of the evidence that was considered and an account of how those data functioned in the committee's deliberations.

Only if the committee finds for the faculty member and the administration accepts that judgment is the case certain to come to an end. If the committee sides with the deciding administrator, an appeal may be made to whatever higher levels remain, possibly including the institution's board of trustees. The losing faculty member may also resort to the courts outside the institution. Finally, if the report recommends against the administrator, but is not accepted, a reason for that rejection is owed to the faculty member, as well as to the committee that made the recommendation, with similar potential for further appeal.

In the end, a committee's report is just another component in the complex personnel processes of an academic institution. Yet even though there is a considerable possibility that appeal and grievance committee reports will not be the last word on the cases they deal with, how they are produced and how well they are fashioned matter a good deal to the well-being of a campus. The likelihood that faculty members will believe that they are being treated fairly at an institution will increase when thoughtful reports are issued by a credible and timely process and then generally accepted by the administration. This, in spite of the fact that the content of such reports is (rightly) not made public. The academic world is a gossipy one, where indiscretion is normal; here is an instant where this otherwise not so endearing trait can contribute positively to the morale of a campus.

POSTSCRIPT ON CHANGE

Where the language of this book is not downright hortatory, recommending what *ought* to be, its tense might be called the normative present. To say, in this mood, that something *is* the case, does not give a report about what actually happens in the world, but what would be *right* if it did. ("One keeps one's promises" is true only because we mean that this is the right way to act and not that everybody always does.) Moreover, we were concerned, throughout, with the way things ought to *be*, as if the reader were engaged in designing a new college or university from scratch and consulted the chapters of this primer on how to organize it.

To address just founders of academic institutions would leave a meager readership indeed! Instead, it was tacitly assumed that readers would consider recommendations concerning areas that interested them and make changes in their own, existing, institutions wherever they were persuaded that what was proposed was sufficiently preferable to what they had. For such readers, I now want to add some practical comments on the topic of making organizational changes in academic institutions.

In everything that follows, life is made easier if attention is paid to the advice of *Maxim 7*, which suggests that the task to be accomplished be formulated with specificity. Sometimes it is actually simple to make a limited organizational change because it is entirely within the authority of the administration to initiate it; the administrators

[7] *Specificity in the formulation of a task fosters the effectiveness of collaboration in carrying it out.*

affected are either won over to the change or are in no position to object, while the faculty is indifferent. But a judgment such as this is easily made too rashly: the administration may be wrong in believing that the organizational change is of no interest to the faculty and opposition among affected administrators can take the form of subtle undermining instead of overt opposition. Accordingly, making the desired change—such as having the graduate dean report to the vice president for research rather than directly to the provost—may bring less grief if it is undertaken when the most affected position is unfilled, so that the next person is simply recruited into the new scheme. Such an approach has the additional virtue of confirming that the change is proposed for organizational reasons and not—misguidedly—because of the particular failings of an incumbent. To clearly determine a faculty's interests, it may well be worthwhile to inform a senate's executive committee (or other relevant body) of the proposed change and to consult that group or its designate.

Few are likely to believe it to be a simple matter when a broader or deeper administrative reorganization or restructuring of committees is under consideration—broader, in the sense that the positions of more people would be affected by any rethinking; deeper, because of the strength of feeling attached to potential changes. To initiate any such changes is largely an administrative task. For a number of reasons, faculties are by and large conservative. They may variously express unhappiness and dissatisfaction, but do not easily translate such expressions into action. Thus, where faculty members believe their malaise to have its roots in organizational problems, they are well advised to prompt the administration to take action. To proceed without such an alliance incurs the risk of ineffectualness. A faculty committee will have worked in vain, and, given the truth of Maxim 9, will have contributed to the erosion of faculty participation in governance activities.

[9] *The number and quality of persons who participate in governance activities are directly related to how effectively they influence conditions that matter to them.*

[11] *Committees whose mission is to perform routine and ongoing functions are ill suited for tasks that require them to move outside the framework within which they normally operate.*

But if the leadership for making substantial organizational change belongs to the administration, collaboration with the faculty is emphatically called for. A special committee must be formed, since, as Maxim 11 reminds us, no standing committee to which housekeeping functions are assigned is suited to think fruitfully about significant change. Care must be taken as to how such a committee is charged and its size and composition must be determined with an eye on the lessons of Maxim 13. Those who would be affected by changes that might be proposed should be able to see themselves represented on the committee considering reorganization, while the group must remain

[13] As a committee increases in size, its capacity to be representative becomes greater, while its potentiality for effectiveness decreases.

sufficiently compact to be effective. Above all, careful attention must be paid to the leadership of such a committee. For if its product is to be a *plan*—that is, a coherent scheme that is sufficiently detailed to be capable of implementation—the group must be led by a person who has the capability of formulating a document that embodies such a blueprint, wherever the ideas in it may have come from, and of steering a course toward its attainment.

As the problems of reorganization are being tackled, the tendency for faculties to be conservative must be taken into account. For colleges and universities, this conservatism is as much a strength as a weakness, so that the institutional changes that are ultimately made should be the vector resultant of a forward looking administration pushing to move into new organizational territory and a more cautious faculty clinging to traditions. The embodiment of such a relationship is to have the administration reorganize *with the advice and consent* of the faculty. Collaboration, in this second decision category, takes the form of having both administration and faculty agree on what is to be done.

Several things follow from this principle of conservatism. The first would be a minor matter were we not speaking about a world in which the word is king. Call it verbal traditionalism or pouring new wine into old bottles. When reporting lines or functions are altered, there is no need to change hallowed titles and committee names to which everyone is accustomed, unless the actual changes are so great that the old nomenclature would be downright misleading. However unreasonably, people are too often put off the substance of a modification because they object to the language that expresses it.

The second suggestion might be dubbed reformational minimalism. Once determined that change is needed, those who aim at bringing it about, keep their eye on the ball. Let them get clear and *remain* clear about what they want to achieve and not talk themselves into turning the place upside down. That place is like a ship being rebuilt while at sea. If the repairs are not made, it will list or even sink, but if too much of the old structure is undone at the same time, a similar danger looms. In short, make all and *only* those changes needed to bring about the desired goal. Desperation is the only reason for implementing a plan so radical that the faculty will neither advise nor consent. And if that point is reached, know that it will take time and substantial turnover of personnel before a new level of stability can be reached.

The last recommendation I want to put forward is purely procedural. I call it the Solon principle, which is itself an ahistorical application of the Apostle Matthew's observation that a prophet is not without honor, save in his own country. If there is a need to overhaul a sizeable chunk of an institution's organization, there is a good chance that its denizens will not believe that any of their fellows have the requisite expertise to come up with a plan. Even when this is perfectly false, this skepticism may simply be a datum to take into consideration. Where that is so, it is advisable to hire a consultant who plays the role of Solon, the sage who devised a constitution for Athens and then departed from the city. An authority is all the more convincing when no longer there to be questioned.

Interactions with a sensible consultant can be fruitful. On the one hand, such a person has a knowledge of more alternative possibilities than most people rooted in particular institutions can conjure up. On the other, both for good reasons and for venal ones, a consultant will be sufficiently sensitive to a client's desires and interests, so as to recommend something close to what those clients have in mind. Credibility may well be the only distinguishing mark between Solon and the folks at home.

The content of this book rests on the claim that for the effectiveness with which it achieves its goals, it matters how academic institutions are organized. Nowhere was it asserted, however, that all's well when the organizational problems are solved. Aside from the ever-worrisome issue of adequate funding, there is the matter of the *people* who occupy administrative positions of influence. There certainly will be occasions when shifting reporting lines or otherwise reorganizing is not the solution to the problems being faced, where, instead, new people must be found to take certain administrative posts. This postscript will therefore conclude with some comments on searching for the right persons to do the needed jobs.

Searches are complex undertakings. When one realizes everything that needs to be done, it is not hard to see why so many of them are less than successful. First, one needs to know what one is looking for and have a *conception* of an outstanding candidate. Then, the searchers must actually *want* to appoint such a candidate, a desire that can by no means be taken for granted. Next, one must be able to *discern* to what degree actual candidates possess the desired characteristics and, ultimately, identify a given candidate as outstanding. In all of the foregoing it is assumed that a sufficient number of those participating in the search agree on these central points and, further, that the search is conducted with sufficient competence to attract one or more excellent candidates for consideration. And if all the above is accomplished, there still remains the job of actually attracting the selected person to the job. Because of the large body of literature on searches in the academy, we will confine ourselves to a few comments only, in the spirit of the preceding chapters of this book.

The appropriate decision category for searches is the co-determinative, where the faculty advises on and consents to the administrative appointment to be made. Where the position to be filled is below the president, the faculty is represented by a faculty search committee; when the opening is that of the chief executive officer, the faculty and other constituencies are represented on a committee led by members of the board of trustees.

Whatever the combination, the first principle to recall is *Maxim 23*, which reminds us that appointments of high quality are made only by people who are themselves in that category. Every effort must therefore be made to enlist the best people to work on a search. (To be sure that they are available for such tasks is alone a sufficient reason to pay heed to *Maxim 8* and maintain a governance system in which faculty participants can be effective.) It is difficult to exaggerate the importance of this point. Since those searching must know and want to fill their opening with an outstanding administrator, only dumb luck will save a mediocre search committee from underwriting a poor appointment.

Maxim 13 is also relevant here. The drive to represent fully all potentially interested parties can easily create a committee that is less than fully effective. And representativeness does matter for the work of a search committee, but it matters much more during the period of the search process itself than as insurance for widespread acceptance of the outcome. To put it bluntly, it does not help to have loud grumbling about inadequate representation while a search for an important administrator is ongoing. But full representation will not

[23] "A" people hire (or retain) "A" people, while "B" people hire "C" people.

[8] Few significant campus decisions are without budgetary implications.

[13] As a committee increases in size, its capacity to be representative becomes greater, while its potentiality for effectiveness decreases.

encourage satisfaction with the result, nor will skimpier coverage undermine acceptance. The fact is that once an appointment has been made, the new administrator will be judged by his or her actions and words and will neither be saved nor doomed by the process that led to the selection.

If this advice amounts to the caution that it is easily possible to exaggerate the importance of politics in accomplishing a successful search, there are still further manifestations of this point. At times, members of search committees, knowing better, permit serious consideration of an unsuitable candidate for a variety of "political" reasons. Yet such diversions not only take time and energy away from the business at hand, but risk starting in motion a train that cannot be stopped before that candidate winds up on the recommended list.

Similarly, but more crucial still, consideration of politics—within the group or outside it—must never persuade a search committee to include on its final list of acceptable candidates someone whose acceptability is anything but clear. Arguments that it is safe to put a less than desirable candidate on the list because he or she will not be chosen anyway assume, without warrant, an ability to predict the future behavior of people known and unknown. There are no sociological laws guaranteeing that every search will yield at least three good candidates. According to *Maxim 26*, it would be a serious blunder if among those who are recommended are some who are the best who turned up, but who nevertheless were not regarded to be really good for the particular job being filled.

[26] The best is the enemy of the good.

If it is misguided for a search committee to recommend someone who is *only* the best, it is disastrous for an administrator to appoint such a person. Periods of searches are unstable interregna. Everyone would like to see such periods kept as short as possible; but discombobulation for a limited time is only a circumscribed inconvenience compared to a much longer period of malaise (or worse) because of an unsuitable appointment. It is thus worth paying the price of beginning a search *da capo* in order to avoid an extended period of unhappiness.

In the 1940s, Fiorello LaGuardia, then mayor of New York City, had a weekly broadcast during which he usually spoke about the affairs of the city. To conclude each of these Sunday morning sessions, LaGuardia solemnly intoned: "Patience and fortitude." He was right; both are needed.

APPENDIX OF MAXIMS

Maxim 1 In academic institutions, the forces of *nature* are centrifugal; organizational *art* must be used to create propensities toward coherence.

Maxim 2 Some means cannot be justified by any end; nevertheless, the only way in which a means can be justified at all is by showing that it contributes to bringing about a desired end.

Maxim 3 Academic administrators do not *manage* units composed of faculty or students, however much they may at times dream of doing so.

Maxim 4 To what position a given officer reports significantly affects the way in which his or her responsibilities are discharged.

Maxim 5 Supervising is work, calling for the dedication of time, energy, and know-how.

Maxim 6 If the organizational chart is the right one, and micromanagement exists, either the supervisor or the supervised is the wrong person for the slot.

Maxim 7 Specificity in the formulation of a task fosters the effectiveness of collaboration in carrying it out.

Maxim 8 Few significant campus decisions are without budgetary implications.

Maxim 9   The number and quality of persons who participate in governance activities are directly related to how effectively they influence conditions that matter to them.

Maxim 10   The whole is both greater and less than the sum of its parts: neither an institution's budget, plan, nor aspirations can be constructed out of those of its constituent parts.

Maxim 11   Committees whose mission is to perform routine and on-going functions are ill suited for tasks that require them to move outside the framework within which they normally operate.

Maxim 12   Choosing the members of a committee in a way appropriate to its function is likely to increase the effectiveness of its operation.

Maxim 13   As a committee increases in size, its capacity to be representative becomes greater, while its potentiality for effectiveness decreases.

Maxim 14   The longer committee members represent a constituency, the more they tend to be drawn away from the faculty members and activities to be represented.

Maxim 15   An office that lacks goals of its own will tend to give priority to getting the process right over getting the job done.

Maxim 16   Where administrators who hold rotating positions are not actually rotated, reality overtakes intent.

Maxim 17   Boundaries are less likely to create solidarity among those who live within them than they constitute barriers for those residing outside them.

Maxim 18   The responsibilities of an office must not exceed its authority, including budgetary authority.

Maxim 19   Decisions obliged to be reached independently by more than one person or agency tend not to be attained responsibly by any of them.

Maxim 20   Doing something twice in a slipshod manner is not the equal of doing it meticulously once.

Maxim 21   Refrain from making rules that make normal business more difficult merely in order to prevent offenses that might be committed on rare occasions.

Maxim 22 Over time, good departments get better, while bad departments get worse.

Maxim 23 "A" people hire (or retain) "A" people, while "B" people hire "C" people.

Maxim 24 In administering an academic institution, act, whenever possible, to minimize the conflict between a faculty member's role as researcher and as teacher/educator.

Maxim 25 To have status without a budget is to possess a gavel made of styrofoam.

Maxim 26 The best is the enemy of the good.

Maxim 27 The obligations of conscientiousness are relative to the moral importance of the task to be accomplished.

INDEX

by James Minkin